Cambridge Elements

Elements in the Economics of Emerging Markets
edited by
Bruno S. Sergi
Harvard University

BANKING SECTOR REFORMS

Is China Following Japan's Footstep?

M. Kabir Hassan
University of New Orleans

Mohammad Dulal Miah
University of Nizwa

CAMBRIDGE
UNIVERSITY PRESS

CAMBRIDGE
UNIVERSITY PRESS

University Printing House, Cambridge CB2 8BS, United Kingdom

One Liberty Plaza, 20th Floor, New York, NY 10006, USA

477 Williamstown Road, Port Melbourne, VIC 3207, Australia

314–321, 3rd Floor, Plot 3, Splendor Forum, Jasola District Centre, New Delhi – 110025, India

103 Penang Road, #05–06/07, Visioncrest Commercial, Singapore 238467

Cambridge University Press is part of the University of Cambridge.

It furthers the University's mission by disseminating knowledge in the pursuit of education, learning, and research at the highest international levels of excellence.

www.cambridge.org
Information on this title: www.cambridge.org/9781009244800
DOI: 10.1017/9781009244787

First published 2022

A catalogue record for this publication is available from the British Library.

ISBN 978-1-009-24480-0 Paperback
ISSN 2631-8598 (online)
ISSN 2631-858X (print)

Banking Sector Reforms

Is China Following Japan's Footstep?

Elements in the Economics of Emerging Markets

DOI: 10.1017/9781009244787
First published online: May 2022

M. Kabir Hassan
University of New Orleans

Mohammad Dulal Miah
University of Nizwa

Author for correspondence: M. Kabir Hassan, mhassan@uno.edu

Abstract: China registered double-digit GDP growth for more than three decades. Recently, the rate has slowed down considerably. The slow growth period, which Chinese policymakers refer to as the 'new normal', has created enormous curiosity among scholars and policymakers. In particular, scholars often tend to project if China is destined to follow Japan's fate. Insufficient reforms in the banking sector in commensuration with the real economy in Japan resulted in an unprecedented financial catastrophe. Similarly, an asymmetric development between the Chinese banking sector and the real economy is observed. This leads to an interesting question: Is China destined to meet Japan's legacy? This Element attempts to answer this question. In so doing, it delves deep into the banking sector reforms of China. The Element concludes that China is not on course to meet an immediate financial chaos, but the country needs further banking reforms to avoid a potential crisis.

Keywords: China, banking reform, economic growth, financial crisis, Japan

ISBNs: 9781009244800 (PB), 9781009244787 (OC)
ISSNs: 2631-8598 (online), 2631-858X (print)

Contents

1 Introduction

1.1 Context of the Study

China is at the centre of world attention for multiple reasons. The prominent among them is the marvellous economic growth the country enjoyed for more than three decades. According to the World Bank statistics, the GDP of China amounted to US$14.73 trillion in 2020, which is more than 17% of the world's total GDP of US$81.71 trillion. Double-digit economic growth for such a long time helped China overtake Japan in 2010 to become the world's second-largest economy following the United States.

However, China experienced a growth slowdown starting from 2012. GDP grew on average 7% between 2012 and 2019 compared to 11% on average in the preceding eight years. This slowdown has created diverse speculations among scholars and policymakers as to whether China is going to experience a hard landing. Krugman (2013) wrote in the *New York Times,* 'you could say that the Chinese model is about to hit its Great Wall, and the only question now is just how bad the crash will be'. Similarly, Wang, Stephen, and Ernest (2010: 4) contend that economic deceleration is imminent for China, but the only question is 'how fast the deceleration could turn out to be?'

Policymakers in Beijing, however, consider the current slowdown as a normal economic phenomenon because the country has achieved rapid GDP growth rate for a long period. This has helped China to reach a new level of development characterized by maturity in skills, productivity, rising wages, and slower growth. This new stage of the economy is termed as the 'new normal' (Green and Stern, 2015; Yao, 2015; Suzuki and Miah, 2017).

The 'new normal' explanation underlies the fact that China has experienced a structural transformation. Agriculture, which was the driving force of Chinese economy in the early period of reform, is gradually losing its place to industry and service sectors (Figure 1). For instance, agriculture value addition grew on average by 3.95% during the two decades preceding the reform of 1978. Reform initiatives in 1978 revolutionized agricultural production. Consequently, agriculture value addition increased on average by 5.3% between 1978 and 1992. As the economy grew gradually, the value addition of agriculture dropped to 3.75% during the new normal (2012–2020), leading to the decline of agriculture's contribution to GDP from 14% in 2001 to half in 2019 (Figure 1). An increase in productivity along with the adoption of modern technology resulted in a decline in labour demand in the agriculture sector. For example, about 69% of the total employed labour force was involved in agriculture in 1978, which dropped to 25% in 2019.

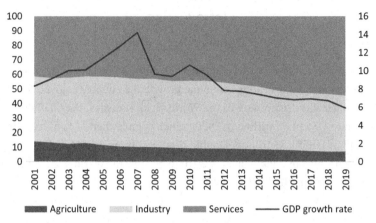

Figure 1 GDP growth rate in % (right axis). Sectoral contribution
to GDP in % (left axis)
Source: *Constructed based on World Bank's 'World Development Indicators' (WDI) data*

Unlike the traditional sector, industrial and service sectors' value addition increased tremendously in the last few decades, which marks the structural shift of China. Industrial value addition averaged 8.23% between 1960 and 1978, which rose to 10.93% during 1979–1992 and 6.5% during 2012–2019. Labour force released from the agriculture sector engaged in industrial and service sectors. Employment in the industrial sector increased from 18% in 1978 to 27% in 2019. Similarly, increased value addition of service sector helped boost its contribution to GDP from 22% in 1978 to 49% in 2019. The rise of industrial and service sectors, which are mostly located in towns and cities, facilitated internal labour migration from rural to urban areas. Only 24% of the total labour force worked in the urban areas in 1978, which jumped to 51% in 2013. These changes broadly indicate a structural shift of Chinese economy and characterize the 'new normal'.

Although Chinese explanation of 'new normal' is persuasive, scholars often tend to project if China is going to tread on Japan's toes (Roach, 2016; Smith, 2016; Murach and Wagner, 2017; Fukao and Yuan, 2018; Yao, 2018). Stephen Roach (2016) seems to be little sceptic about China's imminent fall but does not completely deny such possibility. Roach (2016) states, 'China is not heading toward "lost decades" of Japanese-style stagnation. And yet a worrisome ambiguity clouds this verdict. Japan's fate was sealed by its reluctance to abandon a dysfunctional growth model. While China's embrace of structural rebalancing distinguishes it from Japan, it is struggling to implement that strategy. Unless the struggle is won, the endgame could be similar'. Yao (2018) looks at the similarities of growth drivers in China and Japan to assess if China is likely to fall into Japan's growth crisis. Yao (2018: 31) argues that China relied on export in the past for accelerating its growth and this strategy is closely akin to that of Japan. Since Chinese export growth has already matured, partly due to the declining labour productivity but mainly due to the appreciation of RMB (Chinese official currency), fear remains if China meets Japan's legacy.

There are some striking similarities, despite differences, between China and Japan in terms of their respective economic development. Like China, Japan enjoyed a remarkable GDP growth for a long time, which helped the country emerge as the world's second-largest economy before China took the place in 2010. Real GDP growth rate averaged 10% between 1956 and 1971, which subsequently slowed down to 5% on average between 1972 and 1991. The growth rate then collapsed well below 1% on average between 1992 and 2018. In both countries, state played a decisive role in mechanizing growth strategies. In Japan, the Ministry of International Trade and Industry (MITI) was the catalyst in facilitating the growth miracle by controlling foreign exchange, selecting import of foreign technology, incubating local high-tech industry, dispensing preferential financing, enabling the creation of cartels among companies, and establishing bank-based industrial conglomerates (Johnson, 1982, 1995; Ikeda, 2002; Vogel, 2006; Suzuki, 2011).

Similarly, Chinese growth period is typically characterized by a financial repression, a controlled foreign-exchange environment, and export-led growth. In Japan, the declining trend of young population, required for maintaining a stable productivity growth, was an acute concern in the 1990s. China has started to experience the same problem recently due to the ageing of its labour force. For instance, workforce aged fifteen and above accounted for 79.14% of the total population in 1990, which declined to 68.24% in 2019. The population is further projected to decline in the future, which has forced Chinese policymakers to relax the 'one-child policy'.

More importantly, banking systems were the catalysts in both countries for designing their respective financial architectures and ensuring smooth flow of funds. At the initial stage of their development, Japan and China strategically controlled the development of capital markets so that finance can be channelled through the banking system under the state's guidance. Ogura (2002: ix), in the context of Japan, argues ' … main banks of the corporate groupings have enjoyed great influences over, and have sometimes had to take considerable responsibility for, the managerial policy and funding position of their customers'. Most scholars in their attempt to explain the prolonged economic stagnation in Japan refer to the banking crisis (Hutchison, Ito, and Westermann, 2006; Suzuki, 2011; Nakano, 2016). Most of them are of the opinion that economic and banking crises in Japan are inseparable. Hutchison, Ito, and Westermann (2006: 1) summarize, 'though the depth of the downturn in Japan over the past fifteen years is not comparable to the 1930s, many other characteristics are similar – the duration of the downturn, persistence of banking problems and financial distress . . . '

Similarly, banks played a pivotal role in accelerating Chinese economic growth by ensuring sufficient flow of funds from the state-owned commercial banks (SOCBs) to state-owned enterprises (SOEs) (Cheng, 2003; Luo, 2016; Stent, 2017). In the new normal phase of China, banks are no less important, nevertheless. As per the estimates of the China Banking and Insurance Regulatory Commission (CBIRC), banking sector assets in China amounted to RMB319.7 trillion (approx. US$49 trillion) as of 2020 compared to the USA's US$20 trillion and Eurozone's US$23.64 trillion. Currently, four of the top five global banks are Chinese. These data and facts imply that Chinese economic growth is important not only for China but also for the world.

Historically, banking sector in China dominates the financial system by contributing about 53% of the total financial system's assets as of 2017. According to the Peoples' Bank of China (the central bank), bank loans to non-financial corporations account for more than half of the total corporate funding. The 'big four' state-owned banks – China Construction Bank Corporation (CCBC), Bank of China (BOC), Agricultural Bank of China (ABC), and the Industrial and Commercial Bank of China (ICBC) – provide a lion's share of the total banking sector loan to corporations. Most loans of SOCBs are concentrated on SOEs, which were traditionally loss-making entities. This has facilitated the accumulation of huge non-performing loans (NPLs) in the Chinese banking system. On the other hand, SOCBs' excessive focus on lending to state-owned and state-controlled enterprises has squeezed the opportunities for non-state or private enterprises to rely on the mainstream financial system. As a result, private enterprises relied mostly on informal financial sectors known as the 'shadow banking' or private lending market (Suzuki, Miah, and Yuan, 2008; Yao and Hu, 2016).

Massive NPLs in the SOCBs and shortage of finance for private sector did not restrict the growth of China initially because the budgetary allocation always kept SOCBs well capitalized. On the other hand, private sector growth outpaced the cost of informal finance on which private sectors mostly relied to meet their financial needs. However, the same cannot be expected in the future because it is believed that state-led development strategy has already revealed all its development mantra. In other words, China has reached maturity in terms of agriculture and low-industry-based development. In the last decade, GDP growth rate of China slowed down to about 7%. Even if such a slowdown does not paint a bleak future for Chinese economy, the new phase needs revolutionary and innovative ideas and private sector-led growth (Barro, 2016; Coase and Wang, 2016; Suzuki and Miah, 2017). This requires a healthy and competitive banking sector enabled through substantial reforms in the current system. Is China walking through this path? Are the reforms, which China has already adopted, enough to sustain a stable banking system? In other words, is China potentially crossing the Japan's footstep? What are the directions and possible avenues for future reform if China wants to avoid a potential banking sector collapse akin to that of Japan? These questions are timely and relevant to the development issues of China. Hence, it is imperative to answer these questions by deciphering the development experience and the subsequent crisis of Japan, the most advanced neighbour of China.

A vast literature has been dedicated to unfolding the mystery as to how China has been able to maintain a spectacular growth for so long. However, the literature that explores the role of banking sector in Chinese economic development and what are the future courses of reforms necessary to support a stable growth is comparatively scarce. More specifically, the banking reform in China has received much less attention than it deserves, especially from international scholarship. It is understood that until 1995, before the commercial banking system was introduced, Chinese banking system had been officially repressed. However, significant reforms have been implemented recently in various phases with an aim to prepare the banking sector resilient to the challenge stemming from technological disruption, financial deregulation, international competition, and structural transformation that would feature Chinese new normal soon. These events provide enough dynamics and sufficient rationale for studying banking sector reforms in China and identifying future areas of improvement. This research aims to fill this important lacuna of the contemporary literature.

The research relies on a substantial amount of secondary data to support its arguments. Data provided by some authentic sources including China Banking and Insurance Regulatory Commission, People's Bank of China, the World Bank, International Monetary Fund, Bank of Japan, and so on, have been used to substantiate the arguments of the Element. Data are presented in graphical and tabular forms for clear understanding. Moreover, the holistic approach adopted in this research makes the analysis coherent and smooth reading for non-specialized readers.

1.2 Structure of the Element

The introductory section presents a broader picture of the Element highlighting the research gap that motivates to write a new volume for explaining Chinese banking sector reform, current performance, and future issues. The inspiration is that various speculations, both optimistic and pessimistic, are projected regarding the future of Chinese economic growth. Banking sector, being the lifeblood of business, remains one of the critical elements of economic development. Hence, the information embedded with the banking sector reform provides an important barometer that helps sketch the future course of an economy. China followed its own version of capitalism, which deviates to a great extent from the ideology of free-wheeling price mechanism. Since China has already entered a new phase of economic development and refashioned its economic model to 'market-socialism', a commensurable banking sector reform is essential to keep the pace with the structural change. Section 1 elaborates on these ideas.

Section 2 portrays Japan's economic development and the subsequent crisis. Japanese economic development was unique in the sense that it was practically guided by the state without depending much on the free-market ideology of capitalism. The banking system was at the centre of corporate and industrial business groups known as *Zaibatsu* and *Keiretsu*, which were the linchpins of stability and productivity growth during the heyday of Japan. A bank was assigned as a main bank, the lead bank, for each firm that not only extended loans to corporations but also rescued them during the time of financial distress. Main bank enjoyed franchise value as rent created by regulated lending and deposit rates which functioned as vital incentive for banks to monitor corporate firms. The whole system was mechanized by the state through the Ministry of Finance and the Ministry of International Trade and Industry. This 'convoy system' worked well to successfully catch-up advanced economies. However, once Japan reached the frontier level, state-led development model turned obsolete. Liberalization and deregulation of financial markets disrupted the banking system that could not cope with the fundamental uncertainty. Japanese economy eventually fell into a prolonged financial crisis.

China abandoned the mono-banking system and introduced specialized banks for agriculture, industry, foreign exchange, and central banking activities. All banks were owned by the state which dictated the channelling of funds from the SOCBs to SOEs. Lending and deposit rates were regulated to keep the funding cost low for SOEs, which experienced a boom in productivity and growth. This has facilitated the take-off of Chinese economy. As the economy was gradually growing up, the government adopted various reforms. Section 3 outlines major baking sector reforms in China, whereas Section 4 examines the current performance of the Chinese banking system.

The reforms outlined earlier are assessed through the lens of Japanese banking crisis to sort out future issues that China needs to resolve for maintaining a stable growth. Few issues of Japanese experience are quite relevant to China. For example, Japanese banks failed to manage risks stemming from fundamental uncertainty embedded with technological innovation. Banks in China are expected to face the same but at a different degree from the disrupting effect of financial technology (fintech). Fintech will accelerate the pace of changes in the financial services industry. Moreover, the maturity of manufacturing and traditional industries means that banks must embark on new avenues of lending that are shrouded by uncertainty and credit risk. When Japanese banks exposed to this situation, corporate governance system failed to deal with new risks. Hence, ensuring good corporate governance in Chinese banks would be a challenge for Chinese regulators. Such emerging issues are discussed in Section 5. This is followed by a concluding section that summarizes the major findings.

2 Bank-Based Finance and Governance in Japan

The Japanese capitalism that Ronald Dore (2000) refers to 'a system with its internal coherence' has been the subject of academic discussion across the globe. Epitomizing the super growth period of Japan, Ezra Vogel (Vogel, 1979) published his famous book *Japan as Number One* in 1979. He depicted a comprehensive picture of Japanese manufacturing firms' endeavour in the early 1970s to herald their presence in the global consumer and durables markets including steel, automobiles, shipbuilding, bicycle, ski equipment, cut pottery, and so on. However, the banking system of Japan was also emerging parallel to their manufacturing counterparts. In 1988, seven of the top ten global banks, in terms of assets, were Japanese. Even if the ranking were done according to Tier-1 capital, only one of the seven banks was excluded from the list of top ten global banks (Hoshi, 2001). As the assets of Japanese banks continued to rise, nine of the ten largest banks in the world were Japanese in 1989 (Murphy, 1989).

It is evident that economic development of a country depends largely on how well the financial system can meet the growing financing needs of corporations, especially at the growing stage before firms accumulate a sizable amount of retained earnings (more in Section 3.2). Financial institutions, particularly banks, collect deposits from surplus units to finance corporations. This route is considered an indirect financing route. On the other hand, capital markets provide a direct financing platform where firms can issue bonds, stocks, and commercial papers to collect funds from surplus units. Especially large corporations tend to collect long-term funds through capital markets. The emphasis of a country on a particular financing system – direct, indirect, or mixed – depends greatly on the competitive advantage each mode of finance possesses for mitigating asymmetry of information, moral hazard problems, and economizing on transaction costs. Considering these factors, Japan placed banking system at the centre of industrial policies during the rapid growth phase. Banks supplied a lion's share of external finance for corporations and undertook prudential screening and monitoring roles.

The banking system in Japan, which was the key provider of funds, was a sort of unique institution in the sense that a specific bank, known as the 'main bank', was assigned to a specific firm to act as a lead bank in terms of providing funds and monitoring them. Aoki, Patrick, and Sheard (1994: 3) define main bank system as 'a system of corporate financing and governance involving in informal set of practices, institutional arrangement, and behaviours, among industrial and commercial firms, banks of various types, other financial institutions, and the regulatory authorities'. However, main bank was not only the provider of finance but also held share of firms, supplied management resources and board members, and rescued firms during the financial distress. It was believed that integrated monitoring (ex-ante, interim, and ex-post) was better performed economically by the main bank system than if they were performed by separate entities including underwriters, financial institutions, and rating agencies, for example.

Although this system served better during the heyday of Japan, it collapsed when Japan stumbled into a prolonged economic and financial crisis starting from the beginning of the 1990s. Consequently, the debate as to whether traditional mode of financing and governance can successfully serve Japan in the post-industrial stage emerged (Miah and Uddin, 2017). Responding to these criticisms, Japan adopted various reforms to reinvigorate its ailing banking system and the economy, but to no avail. This section aims to shed light on the developmental model of Japan and its apparent failure. The section serves the purpose of what China can learn to avoid a possible fallout like Japan. Hence, we mostly concentrate on the banking system.

2.1 State-Led Development

The role of the financial system during Japanese economic boom-and-bust cannot be understood without deciphering the relation between and among the bureaucrats, financial institutions, and industrial firms (Johnson, 1982; Cargill, 2000). Cargill (2000: 39) persuasively argues, 'the financial system was an instrument of industrial policy maintained and protected by mutual support, restraints on competition, and insularity between the domestic financial sector, the Ministry of Finance, the Bank of Japan, and politicians'. Although market forces were not completely absent, ' . . . regulatory and administrative directions were more important than market forces in the flow of funds' (Cargill, 2000: 39).

Based on this assessment, post-war Japan can be characterized as a 'guided capitalism' (Yamamura, 1995). State governed business organizations and other economic activities, with the help of various macroeconomic policies, in such a way that serves the interest of the country as a single unit. These guidelines were introduced based on the mutual consent between the state and businesses so that the stated policies can be effectively implemented.

The history of such state-business cooperation in Japan can be traced back to the era of Meiji restoration, although the tie proved to be more effective in the interwar period and cemented further in post-war Japan. The scope of such cooperation included economic plans and administrative guidance. Like the economic plans of Western capitalist economies, state guidelines in Japan were indicative, rather than a command, to achieve the overall economic goals of the country (Yamamura, 1995). These plans helped banks and firms understand the strategic sectors banks should finance on priority basis and what assistance, in case of trouble, can be expected from the state.

The administrative guidance was provided without explicit legal power of coercion, which played a critical role in achieving the rapid growth of post-war Japan. The Ministry of Finance (MOF) and the Ministry of International Trade and Industry (MITI) were assigned the authority to formulate and ensure effective implementation of guidelines. MITI enjoyed an enormous autonomy to oversee the operations of country's all strategic sectors which can be attributed to MITI's capacity to reach a consensus with the industry, the wide scope of MITI's authority over the manufacturing sectors, MITI's emphasis on promotional rather than regulatory policies, and MITI's capacity to rely minimally on formal legislation that must be passed through the Diet (Johnson, 1982). The reliance on administrative guidance entails that Japan adopted a plan-rational approach to development as opposed to the market-rational state. In the market-rational state, economists dominate economic policymaking whereas in the plan-rational state such policymaking is dominated by the nationalistic political officials.

The comprehensiveness of MITI's administrative jurisdiction and the cohesiveness of its internal organization were considered the linchpin of MITI's success in guiding industrial development during the heyday of Japan. Its mandate was extraordinary broad, encompassing everything from energy security to retail distribution, textiles to aircraft, heavy manufactures to leisure activities, and regional development to international trade and investment (Noguchi, 1995). MITI dealt with firms of all sizes and shapes, ranging from family firms to giant trading companies. In a sense, MITI was able to act as monopoly of authority for formulating and implementing policies. The aim of MITI was clear – achieve export-led growth – for which MITI identified certain industries for nurturing. It arranged all required measures to ensure the quality of products of those selective industries for international commercialization. For instance, MITI furnished several innovative strategies to regulate excess competition so that selected industries could secure international competitiveness. In particular, MITI firmly controlled two essential elements – foreign-exchange policy, and corporate financing.

Japan enacted the Capital Flight Prevention Law in the early 1932 to control the flight of capital and foreign-exchange speculation. In 1949, the occupation administration replaced this law with the Foreign Exchange and Foreign Trade Control Law (FEFTCL) aiming to safeguard the balance of international payment on a temporary basis. However, instead of gradually relaxing the system, post-war Japanese administration utilized the law as an instrument to affect industrial policy. Johnson (1982) argues that it was the single most important instrument of industrial guidance and control that MITI ever possessed. This tool of industrial policy was tremendously important because 'control of the foreign-exchange budget meant control of the entire economy' (Johnson, 1982: 25). Mabuchi (1995: 289) describes the controlling role of MITI and the MOF in the case of foreign-exchange control, '. . . the Japanese government stood between Japan and foreign countries and acted as a "doorman" until the mid-1960s. It was able to determine what entered and left Japan, and under what condition. As a doorman, the Ministry of Finance was extremely selective and stubborn.' The FEFTCL was based on 'negative principle' whereby all foreign-exchange transactions were effectively prohibited, except for those explicitly allowed by the government (Pempel, 1998). If the inflow and outflow of capital were not regulated, the domestic system of regulated interest could have easily been circumvented. From 1953 until the oil shock in 1973, the regulated deposit rate remained constant at 6.25% for almost twenty years. Although the deposit rate fluctuated subsequently, it was controlled. It means that the high growth period of Japan experienced a stable deposit rate. To keep this rate controlled, it was necessary to insulate the Japanese financial market from the influence of foreign capital.

Second, the government mechanized and directed the flow of funds as per the national priority. Japan utilized the banking system to execute this plan. Capital market was tightly regulated and kept underdeveloped intentionally. On the other hand, corporate issuance of bonds remained low because of imposing strict requirements such as high creditworthiness of firms, size, appropriate planning of utilizing the funds etc. These polices left private firms with limited choice of finance. Hence, they relied enormously on the banking system for financing needs. Firms' dependence on banks for external finance bestowed state with the power to ration credit and channel it to the targeted sectors. This enabled the state not only to change the direction of industrial policy but also to play an interventionist role. In a credit-based system, it is the state, not private enterprise, that decides the direction of industrial change as well as financial flow.

In a controlled financial system, funding organizations can establish monopoly. In such a non-competitive market, firms are required to pay a higher cost of capital. However, Japanese government regulated the interest rate to keep it lower than the market rate. The Bank of Japan, the central bank, directed a particular bank to become the lead bank or main bank for certain firms to supply the major portion of the firm's total loan. Johnson (1982: 10) notes that the rate of own capital for all corporations in the pre-war period was about 66%, which declined substantially to 16% in 1972. Banks filled the corporate financing gap created by the shortage of equity and bond financing. Noguchi (1995: 275) draws an account of corporate finance in Japan and shows that bonds and stock accounted for 16.75% of total finance during 1952–1960, which declined to 11.2% during the period 1966–1975. On the contrary, funding from financial institutions rose from 60.25% during 1952–1960 to 74.2% during 1971–1975. Among financial institutions, private banks dispensed a lion's share of funds to large corporations. This, however, does not mean that the state control on financial system was relaxed. Large enterprises obtained loans from the city banks, which were dependent on the guarantee of the central bank. In this sense, the government had a direct and intimate involvement with the financing system of the country.

Through this plan-oriented market economy, Japan could catch up with its Western counterparts and reduce the existing gap within a time less than expected. By 1988, leading US companies found themselves in a cut-throat competition waged by Japanese corporations virtually on all fronts of technology from lasers to pharmaceuticals. In 1978, US companies held 56% of the world's semiconductor market whereas Japanese firms accounted for only 28%. By 1986, Japan had surpassed the United States to become the world's largest producer of semiconductors, accounting for 45.5% of the world supply compared to USA's 44%. Japan had come to command 90% of the world market share for dynamic random-access memory (Okimoto, 1989). This industrial development suggests that policy decisions were made in favour of industry considered strategic for the plan-rational economy by the deliberation of government.

2.2 Corporate Finance and Governance

Corporate governance in Japan can be explained by the financing pattern of corporations. In the pre-World War II Japan, firms relied heavily on the capital market for financing while bank finance was modest. Until the late 1930s, banks were relatively unimportant as a source of finance for corporations. Big industrial group, which is commonly known as *Zaibatsu* (literally, *Zaibatsu* refers to industrial and financial vertically integrated business conglomerates), relied more on bond market than bank financing. Moreover, security markets were active with corporations routinely issuing shares to a diversified base of investors. Frank et al. (2014) reveal that the average ownership of top three shareholders accounted for 27.2% in 1907 which rose to 33.9% for top five shareholders in 1937. This concentration was less than that of United Kingdom, a seemingly capitalist country, where top three shareholders held 36% ownership in 1920. This proves that Japan's capital market was competitive and dynamic with diversified investors during the pre-war period.

This scenario, however, changed with the emergence of banks as major stakeholders of firms. Hoshi and Kashyap (2001) report that between the late 1930s and the beginning of the 1940s, banks financing became the dominant source of finance for large industrial firms. This bank-firm tie can be explained by the fact that the government of wartime Japan instructed banks to take care of corporate financing needs specially those which were engaged in war effort (Hoshi and Kashyap, 2001). Moreover, firms found themselves in a miserable financial trouble in the immediate post-war period and were unable to pay the debt owed to banks. Consequently, banks initiated various plans to rescue these troubled firms through financial and consultative involvement. One of the widely cited rescues was the bailout of Tokyo Kogyo, the third-largest automakers at that time, by the Sumitomo Bank in 1974. After successful restructuring, the company was renamed as Mazda in May 1974 (Hoshi and Kashyap, 2001). These phenomena indeed marked the beginning of the bank-based financing and governance in Japan.

Banks' increased role in corporate affairs was further cemented during the occupation period when the occupation authority continued using banks for financing big and troubled firms. Moreover, banks appeared as major players to fill the void created by a virtually non-existence of corporate governance. This extended role of banks earned its long-lasting label as the 'main bank'. As Morck and Nakamura (2005: 439) argue, 'firms' main banks in the 1950s tended to be their assigned banks from the 1940s'.

Whereas banks gained increased influence on various corporate affairs, the ownership of big corporation particularly *Zaibatsu* changed enormously. With an aim to converge Japan towards more Anglo-American type of capitalism, the occupation authority dismantled *Zaibatsu* by distributing their shares to dispersed shareholders (Yafeh, 2000). Morck and Nakamura (2005) show that the shares transferred from the *Zaibatsu* families to the public by the occupation authority accounted for over 40% of all corporate assets in Japan. Likewise, the number of shareholders rose from 1.7 million in 1945 to 4.2 million in 1950. By 1949, individual shareholding in Japan reached all-time high, 70% (Aoki, 1988).

A combined effect of the reform and gradual economic liberalization was that firms were increasingly exposed to hostile takeover threat. As a result, they started acquiring shares of friendly firms as a means to protect against hostile takeover which facilitated the evolution of stable and cross-shareholdings (Miah and Uddin, 2017). This tradition subsequently became one of the salient features of corporate governance in Japan. The interlocking network between corporate groups through cross-shareholding is known as *Keiretsu*. Shareholders of the same *Keiretsu* considered holding shares of each other a way of cementing ties between and among them instead of selling them at a higher price (Gerlach, 1992; Prowse, 1992). This assurance helped corporations concentrate more on achieving firm's long-term growth than focussing on boosting profit in the short term. Moreover, the main bank monitored clients to mitigate agency problems and moral hazard of managers. As the largest creditor, and sometimes substantial shareholder, main banks had definite interest in ensuring efficient management of client firms. Owing to long-term business relation between bank and firms, information collection about borrowers' creditworthiness was comparatively easy. This has helped main banks to establish integrated monitoring by combining ex-ante, interim, and *ex-post* supervision. This system was considered economically efficient as well as effective for mitigating moral hazard problems during the heyday of Japan.

2.3 The Causes of Epic Fall

Perhaps Japan was not ready to face an economically unstable future. With the acceleration of economic growth, asset price bubble started to form in the economy. Real estate and capital market were the primary markets to heat up. The Nikkei Index rose from 11,600 in 1985 to 38,915 in December 1989. However, the unprecedented price rise of real-estate market was incomparable to any other markets in Japan at that time. Yamamura (2018: 106) reports that the price of Tokyo Imperial Palace was estimated to be worth more than the real-estate market of entire California.

If there is a bubble, it is sure to bust. But in case of Japan, the bubble busted suddenly and badly affected the entire economy. GDP growth rate plummeted to less than 1% in 1991, the beginning of the bubble burst, and this sluggish growth would continue for the next three decades (Figure 2). During these three decades, Japan has been constantly searching for a way out of this crisis, but with no success. In what follows, we describe briefly what went wrong in Japan that led the country to an epic crisis.

2.3.1 State-Controlled Finance and Governance Model Failed in the Frontier Economy

The system of corporate finance and governance described in Section 2.2 served well achieving industrialization and economic growth in Japan until the mid-1980s when Japan's industrial policy was catching-up with advanced economies by acquiring technical know-how. This strategy is to be credited because catching-up policy contributed significantly to Japan's high growth period (Suzuki, 2011). In Figure 2, we can see that before the oil shock of 1973, Japanese economy enjoyed rapid growth which slowed down once the competitiveness resulting from the catching-up period was over. Japan graduated to a mature stage in economic development when the internationalization and technological change increased substantially in the mid-1980s. Once Japan emerged as a frontier economy, the bank-based corporate finance and governance lost their effectiveness. Gradual opening and liberalizing of the financial market ushered multiple financing options for creditworthy firms. Notably, profitable firms started replacing bank finance with the retained earnings.

Table 1 exhibits selected liabilities of manufacturing sector in Japan. It is observed that short-term bank loan declined from 16.82% of the manufacturing

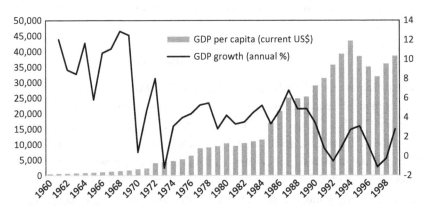

Figure 2 GDP growth rate (right axis) and GDP per capita (left axis)
Source: *Constructed from WDI data*

Table 1 Selected liabilities of manufacturing firms (in %)

	1960–69	1970–79	1980–89	1990–99	2000–05
Short-term bank loan	16.82	15.74	16.82	11.48	9.20
Long-term bank loan	16.25	19.07	12.80	12.74	11.45
Bonds	2.82	2.26	3.52	6.74	4.71
Share capital	14.09	8.50	10.67	14.08	15.69
Retained earnings	11.72	11.01	15.45	20.14	24.37

Source: *Calculated based on Financial Statement Statistics, Ministry of Finance, Japan*

sector's total liability in the 1960s to 9.20% in the early 2000s. Of course, this decline, more than 45%, was significant. A similar trend was observed for long-term loans, which declined from 19.07% in the 1970s to 11.45% in the early 2000s, a decline of about 40%. An interesting observation is that the equity capital declined during the 1970s and 1980s. Data for corporate treasury stock are available only from 2004. Treasury stock for all industries except finance and insurance industries amounted to JPY5.27 trillion in 2004 of which 57% belonged to manufacturing sector. The amount of share buyback continues to rise for Japanese non-financial firms. This has been possible because of the lavish profit Japanese manufacturing firms enjoyed during the 1960s and 1970s. In a span of four decades, the share of retained earnings in the total liability more than doubled for Japanese manufacturing firms. Instead of distributing cash dividends, firms utilized profit for acquiring treasury stocks.

This practice further illuminates that cash-rich firms did not create enough scopes for new investment. Hence, they utilized accumulated liquid assets to buy back treasury shares. Specially, these shares were mostly sold by individuals and small investors. As mentioned earlier, stable and cross-shareholders in Japan were reluctant to sell their equity stakes of partner firms even in the face of financial constraints. In so doing, firms squeezed the scope of outside shareholders as well as regulators to monitor them.

State guidance remained in place at a time when the frontier economy of Japan demanded well-structured liberalization of the financial market. Instead of paying attention to this pragmatic issue, Japanese government attempted to keep the economy buoyant by injecting fresh fund specially by issuing treasury bonds and selling them to commercial banks with the intent to create more loanable funds. For instance, central government bond amounted to JPY1,561 trillion in 1982, which almost doubled to JPY3,000 trillion in 1993. From 1993 until 2002, issuance of treasury stock increased on average by 12% annually. It was expected that if money supply can make a turnaround in the real-estate market, financial institutions could avoid a catastrophe.

However, the frontier economy needed a new model of growth that could create new investment opportunities through cutting-edge innovation. Japan clearly lacked this strategy. As a result, banks were forced to utilize state-injected funds to meet loan expansion target. Hence, banks often overlooked economic viability of lending projects simply to comply with the direction of the authority. This regulatory framework provided an implicit guarantee that the government would eventually come forward to rescue financially distressed banks, if required. Moral hazard in lending and screening was inevitable. This resulted in inefficient allocation of productive resources, leading to the pile up of NPL ratio for banks.

The issuance of government bond had another critical impact on the financial markets in Japan. For example, to float government bonds, financial markets were liberalized so that bonds could be sold at the market price. However, the deposit market remained controlled. At times, treasury bond rates were higher than the bank deposit rate. As a consequence, surplus entities including business enterprises and households tended to invest in treasury bonds rather than buying deposit products. This resulted in the dry up of banks' cheaper and larger source of funding. Moreover, an active presence of government in the bond market subsequently facilitated the liberalization of interest rates in other markets as well. Such liberalization was not well planned, however.

The government still wanted to keep the banking system as the primary channel for transferring funds from savers to investors. In so doing, the government suppressed the capital market and controlled the interest rate. Industrial firms were already in tough competition domestically and internationally. Given the low marginal productivity of labour and higher input prices in the frontier economy, firms attempted to cut costs by financing wisely. Data about the industrial production index (IPI) and producers price index (PPI) provide evidence that IPI increased until the mid-1980s while the PPI remained stable. In the subsequent period, IPI dropped while the PPI remained almost stable. This means that the marginal productivity of labour had been declining since the second half of the 1980s. However, regulation in the financial market impeded high creditworthy firms' attempt to finance at a competitive market rate which would have been cheaper than the government regulated rate. In other words, the repression in the financial market taxed efficient firms dearly and subsidized inefficient firms cheaply. As mentioned earlier, Japanese government aimed at overall economic benefits by establishing the so-called 'convoy system', which encourages all firms to progress together, instead of picking any individual firm as winner.

Despite the convoy system paid off during the catching-up stage, this strategy was no longer effective when Japan transformed into a frontier economy. The government realized the errors of omission that led the country to the verge of transition failure. In 1993, significant financial deregulation initiated that allowed banks to engage in security services and securities firms were permitted to involve with lending activities. Deposit rate was liberalized in 1994, and corporate bond market was freed up completely in 1996 (Cargill, 2000). But it was too late to avert the imminent transition failure.

Moreover, regulatory oversight and government willingness to address NPL problems were absent. In fact, regulators did not push banks enough to report their NPL status. Sometimes, the government helped banks to conceal the true scenario of NPLs (Ito, 2000). This was evident by the fact that the government declared in August 1992 that banks can defer stock portfolio losses until the end of that fiscal year. This direction bought some time for banks to manage their bad loans. At the same time banks found regulatory authority on their side. Ito (2000) argues that the problem of moral hazard pervaded all over the banking industry when the government announced the so-called too-big-to-fail policy. This argument is backed by Figure 3, which shows that the NPLs skyrocketed from 1.6% of the total loans in 1992 to an astounding 13.2% in 1995. Estimation shows that the outstanding official bad loans amounted to 12.8 trillion JPY as of March 1993 for the top twenty banks (Ueda, 2000). This amount was assumed to be much less than the actual amount because the disclosure was made by the bank officials in the absence of any independent auditors' assessment (Cargill, 2000). Until 1998, Japanese banks offloaded an estimated amount of 37.6 trillion JPY.

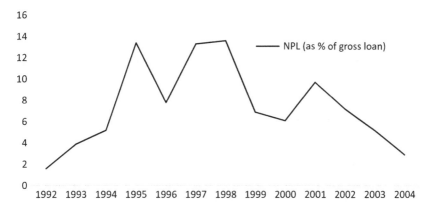

Figure 3 NPL ratio of Japanese banks
Source: *Constructed based on Data from the Bank of Japan*

Despite the mounting NPLs, banks were not allowed to go bankrupt. Few banks and financial institutions were rescued to stabilize the economy. In 1985, when Heiwa Sogo Bank was in trouble due to the bankruptcy of one of its large clients, the MOF managed Sumitomo Bank to arrange a rescue plan. The motto of financial control by the state was that no banks would be allowed to go bust. This policy remained in place until 1991. It makes sense because the problem underlying the mounting bad loans was not merely the result of inefficient management of Japanese banks, but rather, regulatory oversight was also equally responsible.

However, frequent rescue of inefficient financial institutions received strong criticisms from different segments of the country. In addition, the financial strength of the rescuers gradually waned to the extent that further rescue was financially infeasible. For instance, the Deposit Insurance Corporation (DIC), which was founded in 1971, was vested with the responsibility to rescue financially troubled banks. Thanks to the booming economy, DIC was not required to rescue any banks during the first twenty years of its inception apparently because of the absence of any bank failure. However, in 1991, the regulators for the first time in post-war Japan facilitated the mergers of financially troubled firms utilizing the DIC funds. Ito (2000) reports that the available funds with the DIC exhausted by 1995, although the government subsequently injected 17 trillion JPY to enhance the capacity.

The decline of financial and moral capacity of DIC meant that banks were on their own. Between 1991 and 1995, a total of eleven small banks and a few security companies went bankrupt (Cargill, 2000). In 1994, Anzen Shin'yo Kumiai and Tokyo Kyowa Shin'yo Kumiai collapsed, which was followed by the bankruptcy of Kosumo Shin'yo Kumiai, Kizu Shinkumi, and Hyogo Bank in 1995. None of these bankruptcies, however, matched to the events of November 1997, when Hokkaido Takushoku Bank, Sanyo Securities, and Yamaichi Securities failed miserably. In the following year, the Long-Term Credit Bank (LTCB), which was once the posterchild among the Japanese long-term lending institutions, bankrupted. Before the bankruptcy of LTCB, the MOF had attempted a possible merger with Sumitomo Trust and Banking Corporation. The latter decided not to agree with the proposed merger due to the former's colossal amount of NPLs (Hiwatari, 2000). LTCB was eventually acquired by the US-based Ripplewood Holdings.

2.3.2 Competition and Fundamental Uncertainty

Once the regulated financial market was liberalized, financial institutions couldn't cope with the effects of deregulation including that of intense competition. Low demand for finance from manufacturing industries on the one hand and the intensified competition on the other forced banks to look for new lending avenues. As mentioned earlier, high profit during the super growth period helped large manufacturing firms accumulate significant amount of retained earnings. Hence, they did not require additional funding especially due to the lack of innovative ideas and cutting-edge manufacturing technologies. Figure 4 portrays the loans for fixed investment by manufacturing sector. It is observed that the amount of loan reached peak just before the end of moderate growth period in 1991. Until 1991, loans to housing sector and to fixed investment by manufacturing sector witnessed a sharp rise. An important observation is that the loan for fixed investment by manufacturing sector, which is comparatively productive than the housing sector, was only a fraction (about 2%) of the housing loan (Figure 4). Between 1986 and 1990, housing loan increased sharply. This was, indeed, the period of housing bubble. From 1986 to 1991, housing loan grew on average by 12.8% annually compared to 5.5% in the preceding six years (1980–1985). Loan growth to manufacturing fixed investment were 9.5% and 6.6%, for the respective period.

Japan created a different sort of financial institution, known as *jusen* (finance corporations specializing in consumer housing finance), in the early 1970s to cater to the financing needs of the real-estate sector. Seven *jusen* were established initially and provided with the authority to engage in residential mortgage loans under the auspices of the MOF. Although *jusen* was a special kind of financial institution, they were not completely detached from the mainstream banks. In fact, the city banks were the mother organizations of *jusen*. In other words, *jusen* did not collect deposit from the depositors directly; instead, they borrowed from mother banks and other financial organizations. These funds

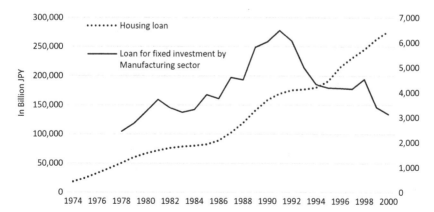

Figure 4 Loans for housing sector (left axis) and for fixed investment by manufacturing industries (right axis), amounts are in billion JPY
Source: *Constructed based on CEIC data*

were lent out as mortgage loans. Owing to the maturity of traditional loan market in the latter half of the 1980s, commercial banks aimed at expanding market to the real-estate sector, competing with *jusen*. It was an uneven competition because the lending rate commercial banks could offer, due to regulated low deposit rate, was at no par with that of *jusen*. Initially, when the real-estate sector was skyrocketing, no apparent problem appeared. The real crack started to unfold once the real-estate bubble busted. About 4.6 trillion JPY, 38% of the total loan extended by *jusen* turned non-performing in 1991, of which 60% were completely bad (Nakano, 2016). By 1996, six of seven *jusen* became bankrupt. Such an epic failure of *jusen* affected parent banks seriously.

Another negative effect of commercial banks evolved from financing small- and medium-sized enterprises (SMEs). Besides real-estate lending, banks also focussed on financing SMEs from the beginning of the 1980s. Like their large peers, medium-sized manufacturing firms did not require significant funds from the banking sector. For instance, the peak of bank loans to medium-sized manufacturing firms reached 33% at the end of the 1980s. Since then, it has been declining. However, banks continued to finance non-manufacturing, small and medium, and small manufacturing firms. Suzuki (2011) notes that non-manufacturing firms accounted for 87% of the SMEs of which 41% were wholesale and retail trade, 24% in service industry, and 13% in construction industries. By the end of 1980s, Japanese economy experienced a structural change. These non-manufacturing SMEs were required to change their business models for successful survival in the frontier economy. However, most of them failed to build this capacity and hence turned risky (Suzuki, 2011). For example, the amount of wholesale and retail trade, the largest segment of the SME sector, totalled 37.33 trillion JPY in 1980 which reached peak in 1991 (59.34 trillion JPY). Since 1991, this segment of SMEs experienced a sharp decline, falling again to the 1980 level in 2009 (Figure 5). Therefore, financing SMEs was a risky venture for banks because monitoring SMEs on building technological capabilities was difficult. When these SMEs eventually declined, banks lost their assets.

2.4 Summary

Japanese development experience in the post-war period owes a lot to the coordination of the trinity – bureaucrats, financial institutions, and business entities. Bureaucrats shared their ancestral root to the samurai of the feudal era and enjoyed enormous power, which they intended to apply to build the nation after the occupation authority left Japan. Hence, the super growth period of Japan can be characterized as the guided capitalism in which administrative

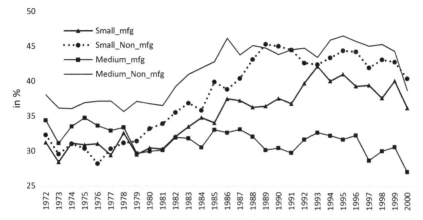

Figure 5 Proportion of bank loans (short term and long term) to total liabilities of small (10 million to 100 million JPY) and medium-sized (100 million to 1 billion JPY) manufacturing (mfg.) and non-manufacturing (non-mfg.) firms in Japan
Source: *Constructed based on Financial Statement Statistics, Ministry of Finance*

guidance directed business organizations towards strategic areas of business development, which would earn Japan a competitive edge in the international market. To achieve this target, the administration considered finance as a controlling mechanism. Financial market, which was comparatively well developed in the post-war Japan was regulated to ensure that finance flows through the banking system. This control enabled the administration to direct funds towards selective industries which the government wanted to prioritize. Government allowed business entities to create informal bonding among them keeping a financial intermediary at the centre. A specific bank provided a major share of a particular firm's total financing needs. This system, main bank system, helped mitigating asymmetry of information and moral hazard problems. In addition, the main bank was able to build a long-term relation with the borrowers that facilitated reducing information collection and monitoring cost. This model of financial system was successful during the catch-up period of Japan.

However, when Japan transformed into a frontier economy in the mid-1970s until the hard landing of the bubble economy, administrative control and main bank lending and monitoring remained in place. Traditional lending sanctuaries of main bank including productive manufacturing sectors became cash-rich and required little external financing as they were accumulating treasury stocks utilizing retained earnings. This scenario illustrated firms' inability to create new investment opportunities when they reached frontier stage, which explains the sluggish productivity growth in Japan. On the other hand, financial liberalization widened the options for creditworthy borrowers to embark on cheaper sources of finance than the bank financing. These events led banks to lose their grip on manufacturing and other stable industries. Consequently, banks were forced to look for new borrowers which were typically high risky SMEs such as non-manufacturing industries and real-estate sectors. At the time of declining economic growth and intense competition, many of these firms were unable to cope with evolving risks. Their eventual failures left banks with huge accumulation of NPLs. Regulatory authorities did not react promptly to resolve NPL problem. Rather, they co-operate with banks to manage those NPLs with the expectation that increased monetary easing would normalize the economy and NPLs problem would be addressed. This error of omission of the regulatory authority aggravated the economic situation instead of reviving it and Japan is still paying dearly for this regulatory mistake.

3 Reforms in Chinese Banking Sector

3.1 Background

The financial system of China was established in 1949, when the People's Republic of China was founded. Whatever it meant to be a financial system, there was only one bank in the country, the People's Bank of China (PBOC), established on December 1, 1948. On the same day, a public decree was issued declaring PBOC as the authority to issue Renminbi (RMB), the official currency of the country. Besides functioning as the issuer of currency, the PBOC also catered to the financing needs of enterprises. The BOC, which was founded in 1912, had performed the central banking activities before the establishment of the PBOC. In 1949, BOC was made a subsidiary to PBOC. It was authorized to perform only the foreign-exchange activities of the country. Another bank, the ABC was founded in 1951, which later stopped its operation. Subsequently, the People's Construction Bank of China (PCBC) was established in 1954, as a subsidiary of the Ministry of Finance and performed the task of providing funds only to construction and infrastructure projects as per the guidance of the state.

At the end of 1978, Chinese financial system comprised only one bank, the PBOC with its two specialized subsidiaries – the Bank of China and the People's Construction Bank of China. Hence, the pre-1978 Chinese financial system was characterized by a mono-banking system modelled after the soviet-style centrally planned economy. The PBOC was delegated with the responsibilities to function as the central bank as well as to implement monetary policy including foreign-exchange management through the BOC. In addition, the PBOC was solely responsible to carry out the commercial banking activities, mainly financing SOEs. However, the mono-banking tradition was abolished through substantial economic and financial reforms in 1978, which opened the financial market and eventually paved the way for commercial banking to flourish. However, banks were completely state-owned and financially repressed. Banking system was primarily utilized to channel budgetary allocation to SOEs. Banks' profitability and commercial viability were completely neglected. NPLs soared owing to the moral hazard problem and inadequate monitoring.

The banking sector again experienced another phase of reform in 1984, when policy loan was introduced to replace commercial lending backed by government budgetary allocation. Commercial banking viability was seriously undermined. Inefficient SOEs turned into loss-making concerns which were unable to repay bank loans. This led to the pile up of NPLs, which in turn, caused a real problem for effective financial intermediation. As a result, commercial banking law was introduced in 1995, outlining a roadmap for resolution of NPLs. At the same time, China officially planned to comply with 8% Basel capital adequacy requirement. However, the banking system remained tightly controlled. Commercial viability was absent due mainly to the traditional style of financial intermediation. More importantly, the Asian financial crisis of 1997–8 affected Chinese banks, but government early bailout saved banks from bankruptcy. The combined effect was that China initiated another round of reform in 2003 with an aim of modernizing the banking system by converting state ownership into private ownership. As a result, big four Chinese banks were listed on the stock exchanges between 2005 and 2010, which marked an important achievement of Chinese banking sector reform.

The global financial crisis of 2007–8, fuelled by the US subprime meltdown, agitated the global economy, and China was no exception. However, unlike their Western counterparts, Chinese banks' exposure to global financial crisis (GFC) was comparatively limited due mainly to the state control of banks and other financial institutions. Despite the fact that Chinese banks were less affected by the GFC, government intervention was required to offload mounting NPLs. Few asset management companies were established to take over the trouble loan of commercial banks. This was followed by other reforms concentrating mainly on regulatory issues, risk management, bank's portfolio diversification, and change of ownership. Restrictions on foreign ownership of financial institutions phased out completely by 2020. Foreign owners can now own completely any financial institution in China. These changes are phenomenal as far as the Chinese banking sector is concerned. This section aims to discuss these reforms in brief.

3.2 Theories of Banking Sector Reform

Financial intermediaries affect economies in multifaceted ways including supplying funds to firms that actively seek external finance. A developed banking sector increases household's trust about a financial system which induces them to deposit surplus funds. Financial intermediaries make these funds available for deficit units such as corporations, for example, to undertake investment. Such a channelling of funds through financial intermediaries helps socialize lenders' credit risk, in which banks absorb risk associated with socially profitable projects by encouraging investors of diverse risk appetite to participate in the formal financial market. In other words, financial institutions socialize credit risk and thereby, play a critical role in economic development. The role of finance in economic development is well documented in the early literature (Patrick, 1966; McKinnon, 1973; Shaw, 1973; Goldsmith, 1985). Recent literature also confirms the positive effect of finance on economic growth (Greenwood and Jovanovic, 1990; King and Levine, 1993; Jappelli and Pagano, 1994; Beck, Demirguc-Kunt, and Levine, 2001; Bloch and Tang, 2003; Levine 2003; Claessens and Laeven, 2005; Botric and Slijepcevic, 2008). The embedded benefits of finance for growth provide a great impetus for countries to initiate financial reforms.

Theories of banking sector reform thus concentrates on how a developed banking system can contribute to the economic growth. Most theories of financial intermediaries explain the role of banks in mitigating frictions in the markets. In the new classical Arrow–Debreu general equilibrium model, market is perfect. Hence, financial intermediaries are assumed to be irrelevant or redundant. This is an unrealistic assumption because frictions such as asymmetry of information and transaction cost are inevitable in the financial markets (Diamond and Dybvig, 1983). The emergence of information school in the 1970s and subsequent recognition of the field by awarding the Nobel Prize in Economics in 2001 suggest that information problem practically prohibits markets from reaching Pareto efficiency. The basic tenet of the information school relies on the logical perception that one of the transacting parties possesses superior information compared to her counterpart. Generally, borrowers know well about the riskiness of the project, repaying capacity, and willingness to pay (Akerlof, 1970; Leland and Pyle, 1977; Stiglitz, 1994). When markets are plagued by information problem, funds don't flow efficiently from savers to investors. Banks can solve asymmetry of information problems better than any other institution by producing information. For example, in the process of mediating transactions, banks acquire considerable information valuable for loan screening, assessment, and monitoring (Stiglitz, 1994).

Prudential screening and monitoring of borrowers depend greatly on the incentive provided for banks. Hellmann, Murdoc, and Stiglitz (1997) propose that in a weak banking system, free competition may erode 'bank rent', which in turn reduces banks' incentive as well as capacity to properly screen and monitor borrowers. Hence, government can provide incentive by creating rent, an excess income that does not exist in competitive market conditions. For example, government can decide the deposit and lending rates lower than the competitive market rate. So long as the spread is positive, banks are motivated to extend loan and monitor borrower's *ex-post*. A regime of positive rent is called financial restraint (Hellmann, Murdoch, and Stiglitz, 1997). Bank-rent works most effectively if banks' ownerships are private. Financial restraint policy is depicted in Figure 6.

In Figure 6, the equilibrium interest rate is denoted by $r0$, the intersection of supply ($s1$) and demand (d) curves in a state of free competition. However, this perfect equilibrium is not practically attainable due to asymmetry of information and transaction costs. For example, the equilibrium 'e' assumes that loanable funds respond to interest rate (price of loans). Supply of loanable funds is greater if interest rate is high and vice versa. However, the loan market doesn't practically work in such a way as the general Arrow–Debreu model predicts. For example, bank doesn't extend loan to a risky borrower even if higher interest rate is offered. It means the supply of loan stops despite further demand exists in the market. This is labelled in the literature as credit rationing (Stiglitz and Weiss, 1981).

Since a perfect equilibrium in a loan market cannot be attained even under the free-market conditions, government intervention in a planned way benefits the

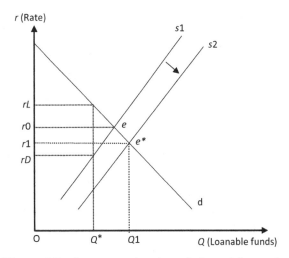

Figure 6 Bank-rent creation through financial restraint

market. In Figure 6, if deposit and lending rates are regulated at rD and rL, respectively, rent for banks equivalent to $rL-rD$ is created. This rent as a 'franchise value' stabilizes financial market and provides increased incentive for banks to monitor borrowers and manage risk of the loan portfolio. Moreover, rents create incentives for banks to expand their deposit base by increasing deposit infrastructures including acquisition of advanced technologies, expanding branch network, and so on. As a result, supply curve of loanable funds shifts rightward ($s2$), leading to the rise of available funds for borrowers ($OQ1$). With the new supply curve, competitive lending rate, when regulation is gradually relaxed, declines to $r1$, lower than the previous hypothetical competitive rate ($r0$). It means that regulated lending and deposit rates yield social benefits at the inception of financial development.

One of the preconditions for the effectiveness of financial restraint model is a stable macro environment. This means that the level of inflation is low and real interest rate is positive. Most critically, governments do not extract rents from the financial sector by tax (pushing inflation up) or other such means. If these conditions are not met, financial restraint turns out to be financial repression. In other words, financial repression persists if real interest rate turns negative and financial intermediaries suffer from negative or zero rent.

3.3 Chinese Banking Sector in Light of the Financial Restraint Model

Although loan and deposit rates were regulated in the post-1978 reform era, China practically imposed a regime of financial repression (Dorn, 2006; Suzuki, Miah, and Yuan, 2008; Huang and Ge, 2019). At times, inflation was higher than the deposit rate, which indicates a negative real interest rate. Figure 7 shows the lending and deposit rates along with the spread (lending rate minus deposit rate) for China. It is observed that from 1978 to 1992, bank rent was close to zero. This means that China did not create any incentive for banks. Obviously, the financial strategy of China in the post-1978 period was not to free banks immediately. Rather, the banking sector was utilized as a formal channel to facilitate the flow of funds from the savers to investors under the close supervision of the government.

China is blessed with huge primitive accumulation (Suzuki, Miah, and Yuan, 2008). Gross saving accounted for 34% of the GDP as early as 1982, which was higher than OECD member countries (21%), middle-income countries (26%), and upper middle-income countries (28%). Chinese government aimed at channelling these funds to SOEs but as per the state's direction. Moreover, owing to underdeveloped capital market, depositors did not have diversified

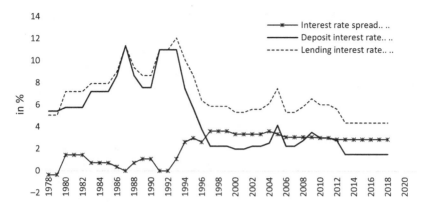

Figure 7 Lending rate, deposit rate, and interest rate spread
Source: *Constructed based on CEIC data*

choices for investing funds and therefore, ended up depositing in banks. In this sense, banking system functioned as an effective tool to collect funds from households and supply those funds to corporations. Bank managers did not have sufficient discretion to manage funds. Such a repressive financial regime creates space for moral hazard for bank managers. Especially, agency relation turns acute in such a circumstance.

Agency relation, in the parlance of standard textbook, entails that managers are the decision agents who make decisions concerning the day-to-day activities of business organizations. However, their decisions affect the wealth of principals or owners because managers possess a widespread discretion to maximize their own benefits, through perks and other such means, at the expense of the principals. This divergence of interest is commonly known as 'principal–agent' problem. Jensen and Meckling (1976) show that the agents tend to maximize their personal benefits even if it deteriorates the value of the firm. Principals are atomistic shareholders in modern firms, and often lack professional knowledge and skills to effectively monitor managers. Principals thus set out various mechanisms to mitigate agency problem. The cost of establishing those mechanisms is termed as agency cost (Jensen and Meckling, 1976).

The dynamic of the principal–agent relation is different for Chinese banks. In China, banks were traditionally owned by the state that aims to pursue multiple objectives – political, economic, social, and sometimes personal. Moreover, the state appeared not only as an owner but also as a regulatory authority. Hence, if a bank suffered from dismal financial performance owing to managerial inefficiency or moral hazard, disciplining managers became further complex because state, as a regulator, possessed the primary responsibility to oversee managerial activities of banks. Furthermore, state could not take its hands off a troubled

bank. Banking reform experience of developing countries' shows that governments were forced to exercise soft budget constraints to rescue troubled banks
(Kornai, Maskin, and Roland, 2003).

This characterizes Chinese banks in the post-1978 period. State aimed to
pursue multiple objectives: financing SOEs for economic development, ensuring equitable distribution of wealth under the plan of socialist state, and
deepening financial development. Banks were forced to extend loans as per
the direction of the state. Consequently, state-owned banks rarely had the
opportunity to implement their own view in making lending decisions. This
resulted in moral hazard among bank managers, who, knowing that the state
supports were always with them, disbursed loans without even assessing client's
creditworthiness (Guo, 2002). This facilitated the accumulation of mounting
NPLs in the Chinese banking sector, leading the sector practically to
a dysfunctional one. Early data on Chinese banks' NPL ratio does not present
the true picture of the banking sector problem because the estimated amount
depends greatly on the definition of NPL. For instance, Luo (2000: 1147–8)
reports that NPLs in Chinese banks could range between 30% and 60%,
although China officially recognized 25% NPL ratio in 1999. Chinese policymakers had to find ways to get rid of this problem and reinvigorate the ailing
banking system. Restructuring Chinese banks through reforms was inevitable.

3.4 Reforms in the Post-1978 Period

After founding the People's Republic of China (PRC) in 1949, the country was
modelled after a socialist state. Under the motto of socialist transformation,
private business entities were transformed into collective and finally, SOEs.
Hence, the production and distribution were accomplished through the SOEs.
For instance, the contribution of SOEs accounted for 90% of the total industrial
output between 1959 and 1978 (Guo, 2002). The necessity for a developed
financial market that could provide required finance to business enterprises was
hardly felt. Moreover, the financial system that existed before the socialist
transformation was abolished. For example, the operations of all stock
exchanges were suspended in 1952 that marked the end of securities market.
On the other hand, the People's Insurance Company of China ceased its operation in 1959. This left PBOC the only bank constituting the whole financial
system. Although the PBOC functioned as a commercial bank by accepting
deposits and lending money, the primary function of PBOC was to fund SOEs as
per the instruction of the central government.

The economy did not prosper as expected under the centrally planned
production and distribution system. Although the agriculture sector was the

backbone of the Chinese economy prior to 1978, Chinese policymakers wanted a 'big push' through a radical change in the economic structure. As a result, heavy industry was given more prominence for economic growth believing on the motto 'a great-leap-forward'. However, the country's institutional set-up was not conducive to heavy industry. On the other hand, an emphasis on heavy industry crowded out the production and distribution of consumer goods. As a result, an acute shortage of essential goods was observed. Moreover, peoples' purchasing power waned gradually. The combined effect was a disaster. Li and Yang (2005) argue that the big push philosophy not only failed to raise the GDP but also had a disruptive effect on agricultural production so much that an adverse change in weather in 1959 led to a severe famine that claimed thousands of lives (Yang, 1996). Subsequently, Chinese planners understood policy inconsistency and initiated a substantial economic reform in 1978.

3.4.1 1978–1984: The Policy of Gradual Opening-up

The reform initiative to gradually open the economy and financial system was launched at the Eleventh Party Congress in December 1978. The motto of economic reform was to transform the country from the earlier centrally planned economy to a 'market-socialist economy'. As mentioned earlier, the primary impetus of such reform was to revive the declining economy that prevailed during the regime of pure socialist state. Households' surplus was almost none under the socialist regime. Hence, banks were not required to mobilize household's savings and transform them into commercial loans. Guo (2002) argues that the lack of private ownership of the means of production under the strict socialist rules from 1949 to 1978 barely left any surplus income for savings. The reform to transform China into a market-socialist economy not only allowed private agriculture at a large scale but also permitted business entities and households to retain surplus they produced. Agriculture growth rate averaged 3.95% between 1960 and 1978, which increased to 5.3% for the period 1979–1992. Similarly, the growth of agricultural value addition from 1978 to 1984 surged more than five times over the previous two decades (Perkins, 1994). In 1978, about 70% of the Chinese population was directly and indirectly involved with agriculture. The accumulation of surplus cash along with the increased economic activities ushered the necessity for financial services. Augmented economic needs motivated China to abandon mono-banking system and introduced a two-tier banking system. This structural change is considered a breakthrough in modernizing the banking sector in China.

The PBOC, which had an absolute monopoly over the whole banking system of the country, was divided into central banking and commercial banking segments. The central banking wing was vested with the responsibilities to monitor financial institutions, issue bank notes, provide clearance services, and maintain overall price stability in the economy. Commercial activities of the PBOC were assigned to four specialized state-owned banks. ABC, which was founded in January 1979, was assigned the task of meeting financing needs of agriculture sector. Subsequently, the ABC was given the responsibility to oversee the activities of rural credit cooperatives (RCCs), which were providing loans to small firms located in rural areas. Another specialized state-owned bank, the BOC, was established in March 1979. It took over foreign currency transactions of the PBOC. The third specialized bank, the People's Construction Bank of China (PCBC), was founded in May 1983 (later renamed as the China Construction Bank in 1996 and China Construction Bank Corporation in 2004). The PCBC took over the PBOC's fixed assets investment services and concentrated primarily on large-scale construction projects located mainly in urban areas. The fourth specialized bank, the ICBC, was established in January 1984. ICBC took over commercial banking activities of the PBOC.

Chinese leaders realized the economic reality and the urge for banking sector reform. Stent (2017: 68) quotes Deng Xiaoping (former paramount leader of China) who stated, '. . . now banks are just book-keepers and cashiers. They are not genuinely undertaking banking functions'. Deng continued, 'banks need to be levers of economic development and technological upgrading. We must make banks become real banks'. Such realization facilitated the revitalization of the financial system that helped mobilizing households' savings significantly owing to the rising productivity of agriculture. Figure 8 depicts the domestic credit to private sector extended by banks and domestic savings accumulated in the financial system. Gross domestic savings decreased slightly at the beginning of the reform because opening of the economy expanded households' choices to consume and invest. The declining trend, however, reversed in 1984 and continued to rise. Yusuf (1994) reported that household savings accounted for only 1.1% of GDP in 1978, government savings 17%, and enterprise savings 15.1%. However, household savings skyrocketed to 18.7% in 1991, enterprise savings slightly increased to 19.9%, and government savings plummeted to 1.8%. This implies that the reform initiatives achieved the intended objective of saving mobilization.

Although the initial reforms indicated the dawn of the rising economic power of China, a host of important issues remained unaddressed that would later be critical for Chinese banking sector reforms. For instance, despite four mega banks existed in China following the 1978 reform, they were fully state-owned. Government had monopoly control over their activities. In other words, these banks functioned as government agents and channelled funds as per the

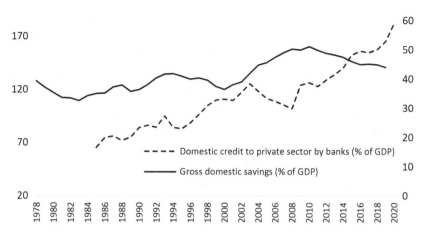

Figure 8 Domestic credit by bank to private sector as % of GDP (left axis) and gross domestic savings as % of GDP (right axis)
Source: *Constructed based on the WDI data*

direction of the state. Because each bank was specialized in their respective areas, there was no apparent competition among them. Lack of competition and the directive lending policy resulted in inefficiency and accumulation of large NPLs.

3.4.2 1984–1994: Reforms Concerning Policy Loans and Commercial Lending

Further reform on the banking system was initiated in 1984 through institutional restructuring influenced mainly by the increased industrial activities, which required foreign-exchange activities and financial services. Annual growth rate of the industry averaged 10.93% between 1989 and 1992. In addition, Chinese policymakers paid special attention to the equitable distribution of income to accelerate industrial production and consumption. Before the Cultural Revolution, a large share of the population lived below the poverty line. Between 1981 and 1992, about 200 million people came out of poverty. During the same period, average per capita income increased by 9.3%. Despite this dramatic rise, income inequality between rich and poor did not rise commensurably. For example, the urban–rural income ratio was 2.37 times in 1986, which declined to 1.62 times in 1995.

Egalitarian distribution of income in the initial period of reform facilitated a revolutionary rise of economic and financial activities. Hence, there was a fear of rising inflation that China experienced before the 1978 reform. To curb inflation, strong monetary policy tools were essential. The PBOC was restructured in 1984 by clearly demarking its role as a central bank with the responsibility of looking after country's monetary policy, supervising financial institutions, and initiating issuance of bank notes. Through this reform, the commercial banking role of the PBOC was abrogated. The aim of this restructuring was to create a competitive banking market by launching Bank of Communications (BOCOM) in 1986, allowing different types of shareholdings. BOCOM was later transformed into joint-stock commercial banks (JSCBs). By the end of 1992, a total of nine JSCBs were established in China. Although they meant to operate as regional banks, some of them expanded so rapidly and successfully that their services were available nationwide.

Economic expansion and the success of regional and small-scale banks attracted other financial institutions. Okazaki (2007) refers Shang (2000) who reports that at the end of 1992, China experienced a surge of financial institutions. For instance, a total of 87 securities companies, 387 trust and investment companies, 29 finance companies, 11 leasing companies, 59,000 RCCs, and 3,900 urban credit cooperatives were operating in China in 1992. Moreover, foreign banks were allowed to operate initially through their representative offices and subsequently by opening branches in restricted areas including in special economic zones. Branches and local subsidiaries of foreign banks numbered 302 offices at the end of 1992 (Okazaki, 2007).

At the same time, the scope of operation of four state-owned banks increased, which can be attributed to gradual easing of restrictions from their operations. This was followed by the diversification of operations of four state-owned banks, which eventually led them to compete with each other and with JSCBs. SOEs were still the major recipient of funds from the financial system. Laurenceson and Chai (2003: 10) show that SOCBs disbursed 91.1% of the total loans to SOEs in 1978, which declined only marginally to 87.7% in 1990, and again rose to an all-time high of 94.6% in 1999.

The flow of fund was controlled through a specific credit plan. The PBOC, in coordination with the State Planning Commission, designed an annual credit plan for financial institutions. First, an aggregate lending quota was specified for the whole economy. It was then divided among the provinces and municipalities as per the administrative status of each province. The PBOC oversaw implementation and effective usage of the quota at the provincial level. Lardy (1998) argues that regional administrations, under the credit plan, often forced specialized banks to provide loans in areas or sectors deemed important for provincial development. In so doing, commercial viability of lending activities was not prioritized. As a result, a major part of this directive credit turned nonperforming. Major change, however, was that the interest-based lending replaced direct grants from central or local governments to SOEs. Okazaki

(2007) reports that the total credit disbursed by the banking sector increased about twelve times from 1978 to 1992. The lending rate was not competitive, but rather it was managed by the administration. Repressive lending and borrowing rates deprived banks in China from enjoying any spread during the second phase of financial reform (see Figure 7).

These reforms brought discernible changes in the traditional banking industry in China. However, the question was whether these reforms were sufficient for booming Chinese economy. The PBOC was not an independent body, at least as per the Western concept of central bank's independence; rather, it was controlled by the state council and required to manage the funding for SOEs. Although Chinese policymakers realized the importance of market mechanisms, they, however, were cautious in letting the market play its due role. National leadership echoed this tone and expressed it in the Eighth Five-Year Plan (1991–1995). Okazaki (2007) argues that a clause illustrating financial reform had a tone that supports the ideology of a planned economy. Conforming to this idea, specialized banks were instructed to prioritize national industrial policy and adjust their activities accordingly (Okazaki, 2007).

Although competition among banks was intensified due to access to new financial institutions in the system, it was not sufficient to create enough incentive for banks to be commercially competitive. This can mainly be attributed to intervention from the state as well as the local government in banks' lending activities. Banks were directed to provide loans to SOEs to meet the production target at the national and regional level. However, these SOEs were loss-making entities. Song (2018) note that about two-thirds of SOEs were loss makers during this economic transition period. As a result, banks accumulated a staggering amount of NPLs.

Economic overheating in China was also a critical contributing factor to the rising NPLs. Li Peng, the then Premier of China, delivered a speech in the First Plenary Session of the Eighth National People's Congress on 15 March 1993. He revised the projected GDP growth rate from original 6% to 8–9% (Guo, 2002). Economic stimulus was provided to various sectors to soar investment in the economy. Real estate was a booming sector. Commercial banks wanted to capitalize on the opportunity offered by this sector. Estimates show that the growth rate of fixed capital investment in the first half of 1993 was 61% (Chinese Statistical Yearbook, 1997). Banks invested in the real-estate sector so much that they often resorted to interbank lending market to replenish cash. Investment euphoria reached so high that commercial banks borrowed short-term funds from interbank market for investing in long-term assets such as real estate. To attract funds, banks offered lucrative deposit rates often as high as 20%. By the end of Q2 of 1993, a crack in the banking system started to appear.

Deposits dried up and commercial banks could hardly manage liquid funds to keep investments moving. According to the data from China Statistical Yearbook (1997), deposits in the banking system declined by 29%. A significant part of the real-estate investment subsequently transformed into non-performing assets.

To get rid of the persistent NPL problem, Chinese government created three policy banks – Agricultural Development Bank of China, China Development Bank, and the Import-Export Bank of China – in 1994 to take over policy lending activities from SOCBs. This event marked the third phase of banking sector reform.

3.4.3 1995–2002: Introduction of Commercial Banking Law

The year 1995 can be earmarked as an important landmark for the banking sector reform in China because the long-awaited Commercial Bank Law was enacted in May 1995 with the expectation that such an act will increase the depth of financial market and discipline commercial banking activities. As such, the law articulated various policies. The PBOC was officially mandated by the Law of The People's Bank of China as the central bank. Regarding commercial banks' prudent lending, the law encouraged market-based evaluation of loan applications by emphasizing on the idea that commercial bank should assess borrowers' creditworthiness and undertake continuous monitoring to enhance borrowers' loan repaying capacity. To formalize the relationship between lenders and borrowers, the law required commercial banks to initiate a loan contract specifying details of loan covenants including loan type and amount, purpose of borrowing, annual interest rate, repayment schedule, and liabilities of both parties if a borrower defaults.

The law also clearly specified the supervisory role of the central bank. The PBOC, as the central bank, shall prudently supervise all commercial banks. To help the central bank, the law required commercial banks to install audit committee with members consisting of representatives from the central bank, concerned regulatory organizations, central government, and banks themselves. The committee shall audit banks' loan quality, balance sheet, and management of assets. The audit committee was also mandated to prevent banks from undertaking any activities that were deemed subversive to the stability of the financial system. Moreover, the law emphasized on the disclosure requirement. Especially, the law articulated that any shareholder intending to acquire more than 10% shares of any commercial bank should seek prior approval from the PBOC. The PBOC also required commercial banks to submit the credit history of their major shareholders.

Like the US Glass-Steagall Act, the Commercial Bank Law of China separated commercial banking activities from investment banking activities. As such, commercial banks were prohibited from engaging in investment banking activities. Moreover, to build commercial banks' internal strength, the law arranged various measures. For example, commercial banks were instructed to maintain an 8% capital adequacy ratio and make some mandatory cash reserves with the PBOC. The central bank oversaw commercial banks' compliance with the mandatory capital adequacy requirement. In this regard, interbank lending market was revitalized by liberalizing the interest rate in 1996. Interbank lenders and borrowers performed transactions at an interest rate determined by the demand and supply of funds. If any commercial bank's cash reserve fell below the target, it could simply borrow short term from the interbank market to meet the capital adequacy requirements. The interest rate was further liberalized in 1998 whereby a 20% floating range was allowed for financial institutions and 50% for RCCs. This change provided banks with an increased discretion to charge an interest rate in commensuration with clients' risk profiles (Berger et al., 2009).

Moreover, the regulatory authorities adopted internationally accepted loan-classification system in 1998 to better control asset quality. The initial trial started in Guangdong province and was later introduced to all commercial banks nationwide in 2002. In other words, the commercial banking law was believed to intensify competition that would positively affect bank's profitability, safety, and liquidity and mitigate NPLs' problems.

However, these reforms were not enough to make Chinese banking system competitive, which was already lagging behind its international counterparts at the dawn of the new millennium. Although the central bank performed various new activities, commercial banks' independence was not clear because of the state's control over them. SOCBs were still functioning as agents of the government, complying with policy lending requests. They were dysfunctional due to shortage of capital caused by the excessive amount of NPLs. Jiang and Yao (2017) estimated that NPLs amounted to RMB3.3 trillion by the end of 1999, which accounted for 41% of that year's GDP. Shortage of capital on the one hand, and the mounting accumulation of NPLs on the other, made Chinese banking system vulnerable to external shocks.

Amidst this, Asian financial crisis in 1997 badly affected financial systems of most Asian countries. China wanted to insulate its banking system from the damaging effect of the crisis. This prompted policymakers to inject fresh capital into the banking system and bailout troubled banks. The government provided RMB270 billion fresh capital to four SOCBs by issuing long-term treasury bonds in 1999 (Wang, 1999). In addition, the government helped SOCBs to transfer NPLs worth RMB1.4 trillion to four newly established state-owned asset management companies (AMCs). As a result, the amount of NPLs of SOCBs declined to RMB1.9 trillion in 2000.

By 2002, the banking sector was still characterized by poor asset quality, high level of NPLs, deteriorated solvency ratios, low profitability, lack of risk management skills, and so on. Figure 9 exhibits the capital to asset ratio of big four banks in China. It is observed that from 2001, the ratio plunged for all four banks. Except for the ABC, asset growth for other big three banks was subdued. With the rising asset growth, the ABC suffered from deterioration of its capital base. Capital to asset ratio was 6.67% in 1998, which plummeted to 1.94% in 2004. This suggests that SOCBs failed to make profitable lending decisions. Return on asset (ROE) of these four banks was close to zero (Table 2). Due to favourable loan-classification system, provision for loans did not reflect the actual scenario.

However, the good news during this reform period was China's access to WTO which facilitated further opening of the economy to the outside world. FDI and Chinese export to foreign countries jumped promptly (Rumbaugh and Blancher, 2004). Increased economic activities not only created opportunities for banks to engage with more financial transactions but banks were required to provide services of international standard. These events paved the way for the next round of reform that aimed at modernizing banking system in China.

3.4.4 2003–2010: Beginning of the Banking Sector Modernization

Following the 1997–98 Asian financial crisis, China's primary objective of banking sector reform was to maintain stability by recapitalizing SOCBs.

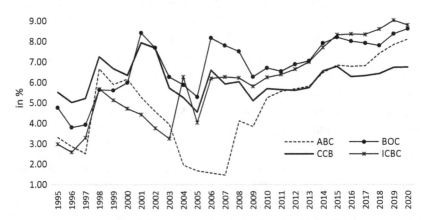

Figure 9 Equity to asset ratio of big four banks in China
Source: *Constructed based on CEIC data and respective bank's annual report*

Table 2 Asset growth, loan loss provision, and profitability of big four banks in China

Banks	Asset growth (in %)			Provision for loans to total loans (in %)			Return on asset (in %)		
	1995–2002	2003–10	2011–20	1995–2002	2003–10	2011–20	1995–2002	2003–10	2011–20
Agriculture Bank of China	13.85	17.21	10.09	1.22	4.53	4.18	0.02	0.43	0.98
Bank of China	5.34	15.76	8.92	2.41	4.61	2.55	0.24	0.90	1.00
China Construction Bank Corporation	7.80	18.09	9.84	1.53	3.96	N/A	0.20	1.05	1.24
Industrial and Commercial Bank of China	6.84	13.96	9.21	0.51	4.19	2.58	0.13	0.79	1.21

Note: *N/A indicates not available*

Source: *Calculated based on CEIC database*

However, the accession to WTO urged Chinese policymakers to enhance competitiveness and increase transparency and disclosure of local banks. The establishment of China Banking Regulatory Commission (CBRC) in 2003 was an indication that Chinese regulators were serious to undertake these reforms. CBRC assumed the responsibility from the central banks to regulate and oversee activities of banking institutions. The establishment of the CBRC heralded the urge for banks to adopt prudential monitoring and supervision. While CBRC was entrusted with the responsibility to accelerate banking sector reforms, the PBOC retained the monetary policy role. This separation of responsibilities helped regulatory and supervisory institutions specialize in their respective areas of operation and maintain independence.

Reform measures introduced since 2003 to modernize banks in China have been focussing mainly on offsetting NPLs from the balance sheet of SOCBs, changing ownership structure of sate-owned banks, particularly, by boosting foreign shareholding, listing banks into national and regional bourses, and offloading shares to public through initial public offerings (IPOs).

Although injection of new capital earlier safeguarded banks from adverse effects of Asian financial crisis, very few Chinese banks were financially solvent enough to compete internationally (Figure 9 and Table 2). Moreover, government suggested SOCBs to go public through successful IPOs. Hence, it was essential to dispose of the accumulated NPLs of SOCBs. As part of this plan, government arranged the transfer of SOCB's 'bad' and 'doubtful' loans to AMCs. Under this scheme, a total of RMB1.2 trillion, about 80% of the reported NPLs and 18% of the loan balance as at the end of 2002, was transferred to AMCs (Okazaki, 2007). In 2004, a total of US$57.4 billion was offloaded from BOC and CCBC. ICBC wrote off US$87 billion, whereas ABC divested US$133 billion in 2008. This offloading resulted in a decline of NPL ratio of SOCBs from 20% in 2003 to 10% in 2005 (Ho and Marois, 2019). AMCs, for the purchase of NPLs, received RMB620 billion loans from the PBOC that, in return, asked commercial banks to purchase special bills issued by the PBOC with the proceeds received from the AMCs by selling NPLs. This literally implied that SOCB's one asset – classified loans – was replaced by another asset – special bills. However, this transfer improved the balance sheet of banks by replacing a non-performing asset with a performing asset.

The government then launched the second phase of recapitalization program in 2003. In December 2003, the Central Huijin Investment Company was created, which received investment from the State Administration of Foreign Exchange (SAFE). Huijin immediately injected US$22.5 billion each for BOC and CCBC in December 2003. ICBC received US$15 billion in April 2005 and ABC received US$19 billion in 2009 from Huijin. Between 1998 and 2005, government mechanized US$95 billion capital injection to the banking system, about 10% of the central government's revenue for the same period (Okazaki, 2007). The primary reason of bailout SOCBs was to retain the ownership and control over them by the state so that funds can be fed to the growing economy.

Besides writing off NPLs and injecting fresh capital, the government intended to transform SOCBs into modern financial enterprises with joint-stock ownership. As such, the CBRC issued a rule revising and raising the bar for foreign share-ownership on Chinese financial institution from 15% to 20%. Moreover, SOCBs were instructed to attract foreign investors for possible joint-stock ownership. In their bids to attract foreign partners, three banks were instantly successful. CCBC received US$3 billion by selling a 9.9% stake of the bank to Bank of America. Royal Bank of Scotland (RBS) invested an estimated amount of US$3.1 billion for a 10% stake in BOC. RBS is the first foreign bank that owned 51% ownership of a China joint venture in 2018. Goldman Sachs partnered with ICBC paying an estimated US$2.58 billion in January 2006. As at the end of 2006, a total of thirty foreign entities acquired shares of twenty-one Chinese commercial banks for an estimated amount of US$19 billion.

The government also encouraged banks to list them in bourses. Initially banks were encouraged to list them in foreign markets. This policy was driven by the perception that disclosure and transparency requirements would be much stronger in foreign bourses than in the recently developed local exchanges. Hence, banks' attempt to list them in foreign bourses would help achieve governance and management reform in banks intended by Chinese regulators. As a result, BOCOM and Construction Bank of China listed and offered stocks on the Hong Kong Stock Exchanges. Following this, ICBC and BOC were listed in the Shanghai Stock Exchange and the Hong Kong Stock Exchange in 2006. Market responded positively to Chinese SOCBs' bid to go public. For instance, ICBC appeared to be the largest bank in the world in 2007. In 2010, ABC issued shares to public, which was the largest IPOs of the world at that time.

It was time to focus on good corporate governance. Hence, the CBRC developed good corporate governance code by identifying ten specific requirements that indicate strong corporate governance. Furthermore, banks' performance index was devised by including seven performance indicators. These measures helped CBRC track the pace of whether a bank is gradually adopting good corporate governance practices and strives for better performance. In 2006, the CBRC issued the Guideline on the Corporate Governance Reforms and Supervision of State-owned Commercial Banks to further improve SOCBs' corporate governance and enhance their internal restructuring.

Table 3 Loan and asset growth of big four Chinese banks

	Loan growth in %			Asset growth in %		
	Pre-GFC	**GFC**	**Post-GFC**	**Pre-GFC**	**GFC**	**Post-GFC**
ABC	13.33	13.20	12.92	15.89	18.54	11.36
BOC	10.81	26.16	10.51	11.51	20.01	10.45
CCBC	11.92	19.29	13.14	17.62	18.56	11.12
ICBC	4.68	17.43	12.48	12.89	15.02	10.49

Source: *calculated based on CEIC data*

3.4.5 2011–Present: Post-GFC Reform

The GFC, triggered by the US subprime mortgage crisis, wreak havoc on financial institutions worldwide. It is often thought that the GFC did not hit Chinese economy to a great extent. Statistics shows that China recorded a 9.6% and 9.2% GDP growth rate in 2008 and 2009, respectively, whereas advanced economies suffered a negative GDP growth rate at the same time. However, the adverse effect of GFC on China was considerably stronger than is often thought. For example, GDP growth rate was 14.2% in 2007 which declined by one-third in 2008. The capital market crashed in October 2007, slashing more than two-thirds of its pre-crisis market value (Schmidt, 2009). Banking sector's asset growth kept rising during the GFC. Table 3 reports average loan and asset growth of big four banks in pre-, during, and post-GFC periods. The period 2007–2010 was considered the GFC period. As such, pre- and post-GFC constitute four years each. It is observed that both assets and loans of big four Chinese banks increased substantially during the GFC. However, the equity to asset ratio (Figure 9) shows a sharp decline in 2007, although a reversal was observed in 2009. This anomaly can be explained by the fact that the government instructed banks to continue their expansionary lending activities so that the negative effect of GFC could be restricted. The depletion of banks equity capital was later compensated by offloading NPLs through government arrangement.

Moreover, as mentioned earlier, the real-estate sector was on course to boom. The GFC caused early bust of a potential bubble. China's export growth turned negative from October 2008 to December 2009, the worst decline (more than 20%) was experienced in the mid-2009 (Li, Willett, and Zhang, 2012).

China aimed for a quick recovery of whatever negative effects resulted from the GFC. Hence, the country put various measures on the table to reform banking and financial systems further. The aim of these reforms was to manage financial risk effectively, enhance competitiveness of banking as well as non-banking financial institutions, deepen financial intermediation through financial inclusion, and strengthen corporate governance. Keeping this in mind, China launched a pilot program on universal banking model in 2010. The model suggested commercial banks to diversify their asset portfolio in other areas of finance including insurance, specialized consumer finance, trust finance, asset management, and so on. As a result, commercial banks either established their own segment of investment, trust, and insurance companies or invested in other companies of similar sort.

Although the SOCBs and JSCBs were hit hard by the GFC compared to small- and medium-sized banks, which were much less exposed to international transactions, the former classes of banks were able to raise required capital from national and international investors. However, small- and medium-sized banks clearly lacked this opportunity. Also, unlike their larger counterparts, small- and medium-sized banks encountered various problems unleashed by financial liberalization. For instance, interest rate liberalization caused serious trouble for small-scale banks because they couldn't successfully compete with larger peers. Large banks can materialize economies of scale and other advantages offered by advanced technologies. As a result, small banks suffered from financial disintermediation and their financial strength eroded gradually in the post-GFC period. Hence their revival was essential especially for financial inclusion because small banks mainly operated in rural and suburban areas. Reform measures in the 'new normal' put special attention to reviving small- and medium-scale banks by improving financial stability, installing better governance, and prohibiting banks from excessive risk-taking.

As a first step, government focussed on replenishing capital base of small- and medium-sized banks. As such, the central banks asked AMCs to recapitalize them through private initiatives, where possible. To facilitate this move, the government allowed private capital to enter the banking sector. In 2014, regulatory authority started a pilot program to establish five privately funded banks. At the beginning of 2015, these private banks opened their business to serve customers. Since then, private capital in the banking sector has turned into an integral part of the system. Private capital was essential not only for supplying capital but also for improving corporate governance of banks.

Further reform concentrated on exchange rate and interest rate liberalization. The central bank increased the daily trading fluctuation of RMB foreign exchange from 0.5% to 1% in April. The band was further doubled in March 2014, yielding more room for the market to determine RMB exchange rate. In the same year, the central bank unfolded a plan for companies established in the free trade zone to borrow offshore without restraint. This led to the slicing of borrowing costs for firms in the free trade zone. Moreover, the floor and ceiling on foreign currency deposit in the free zone were abolished gradually. Regarding interest rate, China introduced the prime interest rate – determined as the weighted average cost of least-risky corporate customers of nine largest domestic commercial banks (Feyzioglu, Porter, and Takáts, 2009). The prime rate replaced the traditional benchmark rate applied before as a base rate for commercial banks' lending. Such a change was perceived to widen the discretion of large commercial banks in determining rates on loans.

Another remarkable change was the introduction of deposit insurance scheme (DIS) in China for the first time in May 2015. The scheme provides basic security for the depositors up to a certain limit in case of banks' default. Under the DIS, deposit made by individuals and business entities up to RMB500,000 per bank is insured. Before this scheme, government had provided an implicit guarantee for all deposits. Hence, activation of DIS was an act of shifting government implicit guarantee to banks as well as depositors (Yamori and Sun, 2019). On the one hand, banks must maintain their reputation and offer competitive deposit rates to attract depositors. On the other hand, depositors need to scrutinize stability and default risks of banks where they want to place their deposits. This reform is believed to widen the role of markets in the banking sector of China.

3.5 Summary

China initiated various reforms in the post-1978 period. The mono-banking system was replaced by commercial banking, although financial institutions were strongly controlled by the state which tightly regulated the deposit and lending rates. Moreover, loans were directed to SOEs. Profitability of SOEs was not the primary focus; rather, achieving productivity by making funds available for SOEs was emphasized. From the perspective of the financial restraint model, zero or negative rent did not create any incentive for commercial banks to be efficient. Moral hazard problem and inadequate monitoring characterized the SOEs and SOCBs. Mounting NPLs in the banking system turned banks functionally ineffective. The government managed to offload NPLs first by transferring policy loans to newly created three policy banks and subsequently by creating and shifting NPLs to four AMCs.

The introduction of Commercial Bank Law emphasized on disciplining banks by enhancing disclosure and transparency. The law encouraged banks to focus on market-based lending practices. Moreover, China's accession to WTO opened opportunities for further reform. The aim of the Chinese government was to restructure ownership of Chinese banks by listing and offloading shares of SOCBs, which was successful. Foreign ownership threshold for Chinese financial institutions abolished completely by 2020. By introducing DIS, the government conveyed the message that state's implicit guarantee on deposit amount is no longer available. Hence, depositors must assess bank's credibility before trusting with their money. Considering the history of Chinese repressive financial system, these reforms' initiatives are praiseworthy and necessary. However, a question remains if the reforms accomplished so far are sufficient to prepare the Chinese banking system for the new normal. This is the theme of Sections 4 and 5

4 Current Performance of Chinese Banking Sector

In Section 3, we have analysed major reforms that China has adopted to modernize its banking system. No doubt, these reforms help draw a comparatively stable picture of the country's banking system at least for now. Banks' NPLs have decreased substantially, and profitability increased to a satisfactory level. Moreover, a structural change in the financial system has taken place where bond and stock markets are gradually taking the place of banks. This means that financial system breadth is expanding, providing firms with multifaceted financing options. It is worth shedding a light briefly on the recent performance of Chinese banks as well as on the structural transformation the financial system has experienced recently.

4.1 Change in the Financial Structure

The financial sector of China has transformed enormously in the last few years, turning itself into a financial superpower. Financial depth of China is now comparable to other financially advanced economies including Japan, the United Kingdom, the United States, and so on. For instance, the circulation of broad money (M2), which indicates the financial depth, has been increasing in China since 2008 when it exceeded the United Kingdom in terms of M2. It is observed from the Figure 10 that the broad money supply in China during the reported period (2001–2020), has always been higher than that of the United States and United Kingdom but remained below Japan. This suggests that China has already achieved a remarkable level of financial depth.

Banking sector still dominates the financial system of China. In 2020, banking sector's assets amounted to US$49.5 trillion, which is more than double of the total banking sector's assets of the United States, US$24 trillion. However, the market share of banking sector is in declining trend. In 1992, banking sector assets accounted for 91.53% of the total financial system's

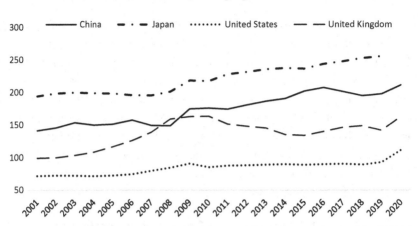

Figure 10 Broad money supply (M2) of some selected countries (as % of GDP)
Source: *Constructed based on WDI data*

assets, which declined to 52.75% in 2017 (Figure 11). The decline of banking sector's share is due to the rise of capital market, especially bond and stock markets. If the broad money circulation indicates financial depth, the penetration of capital market indicates the breadth of financial market. Recent data show that financial breadth of China has been expanding parallel to the financial depth. Two stock exchanges – Shanghai and Shenzhen – were established in 1990 and 1991, respectively. They are well functioning as a direct financing route and provide effective platforms for firms, government, and investors. Although the capital market witnessed a few boom-and-bust episodes during the first few years (2001 and 2007), the market was stabilized subsequently (Figure 11). China Securities Regulatory Commission was established in 1992 as a separate entity to oversee the compliance of regulations and protect the interest of all parties in the market.

Like the capital market, the bond market has been rising significantly. Chinese bond market amounted to US$11.895 trillion, which is the third largest in the world, following the United States and Eurozone. However, the journey of the sector was not smooth. Due to the lack of supervisory experience, the bond market was initially mismanaged. Several bonds issued by SOEs defaulted. This was followed by the suspension of the issue for a while. After revitalizing the market, corporations and SOEs were allowed to issue bonds again. However, corporate bonds constitute more than one-fifth (21.1%) of the total outstanding bonds. Local governments are the dominant issuers of bonds (28%) followed by the central government (21%). In 1993, outstanding bond value of private and public issuers was almost equal (51% and 49%). However, private issuers made an inroad in the bond market. Private bond holding

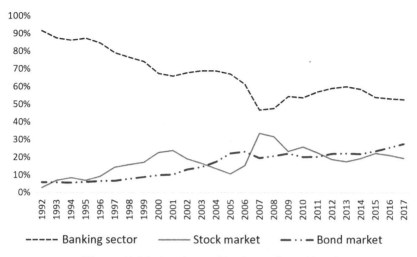

--- --- Banking sector ———— Stock market — ·· — Bond market

Figure 11 Market share of bank, stock, and bond
Source: *Constructed based on IMF data*

accounts for 62% of the total bond outstanding in 2017 and the remaining 38% is held by different entities of government.

However, in the last six years, government bonds outweighed private bonds by a good margin. Table 4 shows the new issue of bonds in China. Bonds issued by commercial banks and enterprises accounted for less than 10%, whereas government bonds dominated the market and accounted for about 60% of the new issue. Among government bonds, local government accounted for about one-third of the new issue. There are some instances of foreign bonds in China, but the denomination is insignificant. Although new issue increases gradually, diversity of investors in the bond market is not achieved yet. About 70% of the outstanding bonds are held by commercial banks (Luo, 2016). Other institutional investors including insurance companies, mutual funds, venture capital, and so on, hold a good percentage of outstanding bonds. Recently, foreign holdings of Chinese bonds increased significantly after the removal of restrictions. This suggests that a structural transformation of Chinese financial system is in the making.

4.2 Banking Sector's Performance

As mentioned before, banking sector remains a vital source of finance for firms. Banking sector assets increased from RMB268 trillion in 2018 to RMB336 trillion as of the second quarter of 2019 (Table 5). Banks credit as percentage of GDP shows a steady rise. For instance, credit as percentage of GDP was 126% in 2002, which declined to 102% in 2008 and rebounded to rise again to 182.43% in 2020.

Table 4 Issue of bonds by various entities (amounts are in billion RMB, except %)

	Total issue	Central govt. (excluding local govt.)	%	Local govt.	%	Commercial banks	%	Enterprise	%
2015	9,875	1988	20	3835	39	201	2	343	3
2016	14,140	2946	21	6046	43	366	3	592	4
2017	13,580	3866	28	4358	32	657	5	373	3
2018	13,664	3541	26	4165	30	1009	7	240	2
2019	15,294	4009	26	4362	29	1588	10	361	2
2020	21,848	7017	32	6444	29	1935	9	393	2

Source: *Calculated based on CEIC data*

Table 5 Selected performance indicators of banking sector

	2018	2019	2020	2021 (Q2)
Banking sector assets (in trillion RMB)	268	290	319.7	336
NPLs (% of total loans)	1.83	1.86	1.84	1.76
Capital adequacy ratio (%)	11.03	11.95	12.04	11.91
Liquidity ratio (%)	55.31	58.46	58.41	57.62
Gross domestic savings (% of GDP)	44.94	43.98	N/A	N/A
Domestic credit to private sector (% of GDP)	157.81	165.39	182.43	N/A

Note: *N/A indicates not available*
Source: *China Banking and Insurance Regulatory Commission (CBIRC) and WDI*

Since 2001, credit to private sector increased on average by 2.9% annually over the GDP growth rate. Thanks to the saving habit of the people of China, banking sector has been able to attract deposits from the surplus sector of the economy. The country is renowned for primitive accumulation (Suzuki, Miah, and Yuan, 2008). Domestic savings increased from 38% of the GDP in 2001 to 44% in 2019. As the country has entered a new normal phase, households have increased consumption of durable and luxury products with the rise of national income. Hence, savings rate experienced a decline in the past few years. In 2010, domestic saving accounted for 51% of the GDP, which declined to 44% in 2019, an average annual decline of 1.64% over the GDP growth rate.

One of the vital signs of the banking sector risk is the NPL. As mentioned in Section 3, the government of China transferred a massive amount of non-performing loans of SOCBs to AMCs in 2004, which drastically reduced the ratio of NPLs. Since then, the NPL ratio was in declining trend. Between 2010 and 2013, the NPL ratio reached its lowest point, around 1%. Since then, the NPL ratio has been increasing but remains steady at less than 2% until Q2 of 2020. Another critical factor that indicates the vulnerability of banks is the capital adequacy ratio (CAR). Although BASEL III requires banks to maintain 8% capital on risk-weighted assets, banks in China are in line with this regulation. Their CAR varied within the range of 11–12% in the last couple of years. Likewise, short-term solvency, indicated by liquidity ratio, also remains well above 50% throughout the years.

Bank's strategy to cut NPL ratio helped them register a sizable profit in the post-reform period. For instance, return on asset (ROA) was lower between

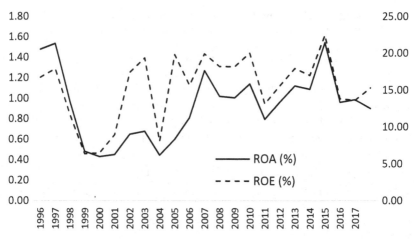

Figure 12 Return on asset (left axis, in %) and return on equity (right axis, in %)
Source: *Authors' construction based on IMF data*

1999 and 2004 (left axis of Figure 12). The offloading of NPL helped banks stabilize the ROA before it plunged again in 2016. A similar trend was noted for return on equity (ROE), which shows a fluctuation between 1996 and 2017. Financial repression (see Section 3 for detail), which characterized the financial system of China between 1978 and 1994, did not allow banks to enjoy profit. The repressive system was lifted in 1995, by introducing commercial banking system. Consequently, the interest rate spread, lending rate minus deposit rate, jumped from zero percentage in 1992 to about 3% in 1995. This has helped banks capture profit in the post-1995 era, although directive and policy lending still characterized the system.

5 Is China Set to Follow Japan's Footstep?

The answer to the question if China is likely to follow Japan's footstep depends more on what awaits the future of Chinese banks than what China has already achieved in terms of banking sector reforms. There are some issues that the Peoples' Republic must address soon. Asymmetric reform, in which the degree of financial reform lags way behind the economic reform, may hamper China's future progress. Furthermore, Chinese RMB has been kept artificially depreciated which provides an advantage to the domestic exporters. However, like the Plaza accord of Japan in 1985, China can expect intense pressure to liberalize her foreign-exchange market, possibly by abolishing regulatory and administrative restrictions. Current trade war between China and the United States hints such possibility to a great extent. This means that the resilience of the Chinese banking system would be put into a real litmus test once the market is fully liberalized.

Table 6 Shareholders of big four Chinese banks (in %)

Shareholders	ABC	ICBC	BOC	CCBC
Central Huijin (state-owned)	40.03	34.71	64.02	57.11
HKSCC (foreign legal entity)	8.73	24.18	27.82	37.54
MOF	35.29	31.14	-	-
Social Security Fund (state-owned)	6.72	3.46		
China Securities Finance Corp. (state-owned)	0.53	0.68	2.92	0.88
Others		8.70	8.83	5.24	4.47
Total	100	100	100	100

Source: *Calculated based on the annual reports of respective banks*

Moreover, the penetration of bond and stock markets, government's policy of inclusive finance, incompatible corporate governance model, and the galloping rise of fintech market are some of the critical factors that may appear as threats to the thriving commercial banking sector in China. This may also change bank's risk appetite, which will have an important repercussion for the sustainability of Chinese banks. The following subsections cover these issues in detail.

5.1 Asymmetric Reform and Political Uncertainty

Although China has adopted drastic policy measures to keep its growing economy vibrant, 'asymmetric reform' remains one of the critical concerns for Chinese leaders. In other words, Chinese policymakers have put a laudable endeavour to reform product and service markets. However, a parallel reform for financial market was not achieved. Major shares of SOCBs, which traditionally played a critical role in financing Chinese SOEs, are owned by the state despite recent reforms. It is observed in Table 6 that government ownerships in big four Chinese banks range between 60% and 90%. Although the grip of SOCBs on the financial system has eroded over the years, they control 41% of the banking sector's assets as of 2019 (Matthews and Zhiguo, 2020). On the other hand, city commercial banks are mostly owned by the local government, although a minor stake of them is owned by foreign investors. This means that government influence on financing SOEs through SOCBs is likely to remain unchanged.

Chinese SOEs are integral parts of the economy. In 2021, 143 Chinese companies made their places in the Fortune Global 500 list of which eighty-two firms were SOEs. This number is much higher than the combined SOEs from the rest of the world that have been able to secure their places in the list. This means that Chinese SOEs are not only critical for the Chinese economy but

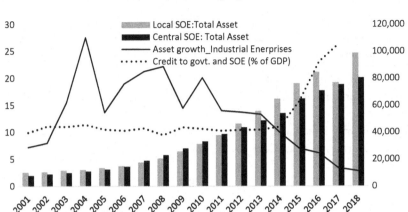

Figure 13 Left axis: Asset growth of industrial enterprises and credit to government holding and state-owned enterprises (in %). Right axis: Asset of central and local government (in billion RMB)

Source: *Constructed based on CEIC (except credit to government holding and state-owned enterprises which was collected from IMF)*

also important for the world economy. Although the number of Chinese SOEs declined over the years from 262,000 in 1997 to 173,000 in 2016, central and local government assets skyrocketed from RMB16.67 trillion in 2001 to RMB178.75 trillion as of December 2018 (Figure 13). Asset of local government exceeded the asset of the central government at the start of the new normal (2012) which entails that economic reform, which is aimed at decentralizing economic activities, is on course to achieve its objective. Most SOEs are listed in the Shanghai and Shenzhen stock exchanges and account for more than half (52%) of the total market capitalization of these two exchanges.

These statistics imply that Chinese SOEs are still significant for the Chinese economy and SOCBs would keep lending to those enterprises. Figure 13 reports that credit to government and SOEs was stable at about 10% of the country's GDP between 2001 and 2014. In the subsequent period, bank lending to government and SOEs rose tremendously which can be explained partly by the declining GDP (denominator) in this period, but mainly due to government expansionary monetary policy to keep the GDP growth rate sustainable. This suggests that government interference towards SOCBs to finance SOEs is likely to continue in the future which will be a critical factor for banking sector risk and profit.

SOEs are inefficient because of low productivity, higher cost, and lower profitability compared to their private counterparts (Figure 14). Traditionally, SOEs were loss making, which were unable to repay their loans borrowed from SOCBs. This has been one of the reasons for piling up of NPLs in the banking

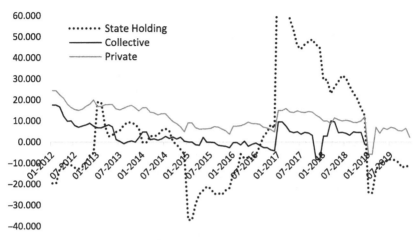

Figure 14 Monthly profit change of state, collective, and private industrial enterprises
Source: *Constructed based on CEIC database*

sector. However, SOEs have shown competency by earning a positive return. In 1997, return on equity of SOEs was 2.3%, which rose to 6.4% in 2007 and subsequently plummeted to 2.7% in 2016. Hence, it remains to be seen if this meagre rate of return is enough to make SOEs competitive in the free-market regime once funds at a subsidized rate from the SOCBs under the government implicit guarantee stops flowing. The balance sheet of SOEs shows that leverage accounted for 67.10% in 1997, which did not change much over the years, declining only marginally to 65.5% in 2016. Figure 14 shows the monthly profit change of state, collective, and private industrial enterprises in China during the new normal (year 2020 is excluded to avoid pandemic effects). The figure shows unstable profitability for SOEs, whereas collective and private enterprises exhibit a somewhat stable scenario of profit. Throughout the period, profit growth for private enterprises remained above the state and collective enterprises, provided that the profit of state enterprises during 2017 is considered outlier.

It is understood that the Chinese government allocates budget through the banking system to SOEs for ensuring employment and social stability. However, allocation of resources by governments is not as efficient as that of the market. Hence, if the government keeps its grip on the financial system tight, resource misallocation may hamper the growth of the country. In the past, government injected funds into SOCBs to compensate for the accumulation of NPLs owing mainly to lending to SOEs. However, repeating the same in the new normal would be neither feasible nor desirable. This means that during the time of asymmetric reform, banks are likely to face an uncertain future as to whether they can make lending decisions without influence from the state. If the answer is negative, banking sectors' reform is unlikely to pay-off to maintain a stable growth that depends mostly on private sector, especially after the reform.

5.2 Maintaining GDP Growth Rate by Financial Inclusion

The slowdown of GDP growth rate of China implies that its traditional growth drivers have already reached maturity. If the country aims to maintain the current or an increased level of GDP growth rate, it must focus on financial inclusion. Financial inclusiveness embodies the idea that financial services, particularly banking services, and credit distribution, are to be taken to the doorstep of rural and unbanked population. Poverty eradication by reducing income inequality cannot be achieved if finance doesn't reach the segment of the population who live at the bottom of the population pyramid. China knows well that maintaining a lofty GDP growth in the new normal would be tough if consumption of durable consumer goods, which typifies an upper middle-income country, cannot be stimulated at all levels.

Chinese government has adopted various policies to attain financial inclusion. One of the salient strategies is to expand financial services to unbanked or untapped population of the country. As such, CBRC (in April 2018 CBRC merged with China Insurance Regulatory Commission and renamed as China Banking and Insurance Regulatory Commission, CBIRC) launched China Rural Banking Services Distribution Map on its website in 2007. The aim of doing so was to increase the physical presence of Chinese mainstream banks in previously unserved areas. In 2014, the CBRC issued a guideline for promoting rural coverage and set a target to provide basic financial services to all villages in a span of three to five years. In addition, government eased the process of licensing for establishing special sub-branches and community sub-branches.

Local governments were very enthusiastic and supportive of this policy. Consequently, they introduced various incentive measures including tax exemptions, tax deductions, subsidies, loan guarantee, and so on. These initiatives resulted in an increased coverage of financial institutions by expanding their infrastructure (Table 7). For instance, the number of ATMs increased on average by 8% annually during 2015–2018. In 2015, the number of ATMs was 77.13 per 100,000 adults, which rose to 97.12 in 2018 but declined during the pandemic to 87.88 in 2020. However, the number of commercial banks' branches increased only marginally from 8.53 per 100,000 adults in 2015 to

Table 7 Financial access statistics

	2015	2016	2017	2018	2019	2020
Number of ATMs per 100,000 adults	77.13	81.74	84.43	97.12	95.55	87.88
Number of commercial bank branches per 100,000 adults	8.53	8.81	8.81	8.88	8.86	8.79
Number of depositors with commercial banks per 1,000 adults	19.33	22.25	25.55	29.18	33.21	36.45
Number of borrowers from commercial banks per 1,000 adults	345.99	385.08	427.96	470.93	504.90	535.92
Outstanding deposits with commercial banks (% of GDP)	154.49	156.65	149.97	144.28	146.37	157.71
Outstanding loans from commercial banks (% of GDP)	97.90	100.93	100.80	103.55	108.88	119.42

Source: *IMF Financial Access Survey (FAS) data*

8.79 in 2020. This can be attributed to the increased adoption of financial technology (fintech), which makes physical branches of commercial banks redundant (more in Subsection 5.4).

Government's effort to widen the penetration of financial services paid off to a great extent. The number of depositors with commercial banks almost doubled from 19.33 per 1,000 adults in 1995 to 36.45 in 2020. Similarly, the number of borrowers from commercial banks jumped from 346 per 1,000 adults in 2015 to 536 in 2020, an average increase of 9% per year. Not only the number of depositors and borrowers increased during the time of new normal, financial exposure of banks also improved significantly. In 2015, outstanding deposits with commercial banks was 154.49% of GDP which rose to 157.71% of GDP in 2020. This means that deposits growth rate exceeded GDP growth rate on average by 0.51% per annum for the period 2015–2020. Compared to the deposit, the amount of loan increased substantially. In 2015, outstanding loans from commercial banks were 97.9% of GDP which rose to 119.42% of GDP in 2020, an average growth of more than 4% above the GDP growth rate. These statistics suggest that commercial banks are expanding their financial exposure to new customers.

Moreover, as mentioned in Section 3, following the economic reform, China introduced RCCs to spread finance among the rural people. They had been successfully financing rural individuals and enterprises until the new millennium. However, financial liberalization and gradual opening of the economy, especially following the China's accession to the WTO, credit unions and credit cooperatives were adversely affected mainly by the pile up of NPLs (IMF, 2018). Their role in financing enterprises and individuals eroded significantly. According to Financial Access Survey (FAS) of IMF, the number of credit unions and credit cooperatives declined massively from 19,500 in 2006 to merely 668 in 2020. The number of branches also declined commensurably from 59,048 in 2006 to only 16,254 in 2020.

The gap created by the exodus of credit unions and credit cooperatives has been subsequently filled by commercial banks. Although the number of commercial banks increased minimally from 144 in 2006 to 192 in 2020, on average more than three banks annually, the number of branches of commercial banks increased on average by more than 1,700 yearly during the new normal period (2012–2020). This implies that commercial banks have filled the financing void created by the demise of credit institutions.

The replacement of credit cooperatives and credit unions with more competitive and sustainable institutions like commercial banks suggests a positive change for Chinese financial system. Figure 15 shows that more than one-third of the total outstanding loans distributed by commercial banks go to SMEs.

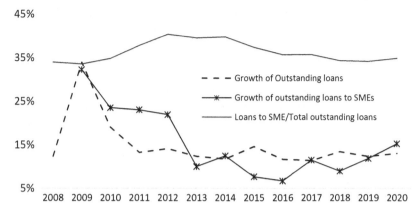

Figure 15 Trend of loan distribution to SMEs by commercial banks
Source: *Constructed based on IMF data*

During the new normal, outstanding loans of commercial banks are in a declining trend and so does the growth of outstanding loans from commercial banks to SMEs. This has kept the percentage of loans distributed by commercial banks to SMEs steady, which has an important repercussion for risk and return of financial institutions. For example, expanding loans to new and previously unserved areas is likely to increase banks' credit risk because the problem of asymmetry of information of small firms is acute. One of the reasons attributed to Japanese banking sector collapse was banks' expansion of loans to SMEs when large enterprises became cash-rich and financially self-sufficient (Section 2).

Asymmetry of information is a typical problem in the financial market worldwide which induces credit rationing (Stiglitz and Weiss, 1981). However, the problem is more severe in case of SMEs because they lack proper accounting records and mostly rely on their informal relationship for lending and borrowing. SMEs in China are also no exception. Yeung (2009) conducts a survey on Chinese bank managers and finds that lenders rely on their personal connection and mutual trust with the borrowers to decide if a loan application can be approved or not. This is because most of such loan applicants fail to provide required documents. This situation hampers bank managers to concretely make loan decisions. It remains to be seen if Chinese commercial banks, which traditionally functioned as an important financing partner for large SOEs, have been able to develop screening and monitoring skills to cope with the asymmetry of information embedded with the SMEs. Commercial banks' endeavour to make an inroad into SMEs and rural markets may appear as an augmented challenge for banks in terms of credit risk management.

Although credit rating agencies can mitigate asymmetry of information problems by providing credit information to lenders and investors, rating information supplied by Chinese credit rating agencies generally does not carry much practical value. Livingston, Poon, and Zhou (2018) and Baglole (2004) view the existence of Chinese credit rating agencies as merely a regulatory requirement rather than a demand for information from investors. Current regulation in China requires all public bonds to be rated by the credit rating agencies. Under such a regulatory environment, credit rating is merely a rubber stamp rather than a true reflection of lenders' default probability. Hence, managing credit risk of SMEs would remain a fundamental challenge for Chinese banks to tackle.

5.3 Financial Liberalization and Heightened Competition

In Section 3, we explained in detail that the government of China has put various policies to liberalize the financial markets. This has an important repercussion for banks' competition and credit risk. According to the 'competition-efficiency' nexus, competition is beneficial for fostering efficiency of banks. In a closed or restricted financial markets, free competition among and between banks is denied. Consequently, bank managers suffer from moral hazard problems because restricted financial market assures banks a sizable profit even if they are inefficient. If entry restriction and natural monopoly are abolished, banks must increase efficiency to successfully compete with the competitors. Inefficient banks will eventually be wedded out. Hence, firms' survival in the competitive markets depends greatly on increasing efficiency.

In contrast, the 'competition-fragility' hypothesis posits that excess competition in the financial market encourages banks to assume more risk and focus on short term gain. Price of loans is not determined based on the loanable demand and supply because as per the 'lemon problem' in relation to credit market, bad borrowers always tend to pay higher interest rate for borrowing. However, disbursing loans to them is extremely risky because the default probability of such projects is high. Hence, banks, instead of rising interest rate in commensuration with the loan demand, ration credit and grants loan only to creditworthy projects. To filter a good project from the bad one, bank must incur cost for acquiring client information and properly screening them. Intense competition reduces incentive for banks to invest enough for acquiring borrowers' information and continuously monitor them because the franchise value of banks reduces along with the increase of competition. Bank's credit risk tends to rise, as a result. If competition erodes banks' lending rate resulting in low profitability, banks default risk is likely to increase.

It is observed that the banks in China faced very little competition from local and foreign banks in the past, partly because of natural monopoly established by a few large banks due to their sheer size, but mainly because the government mechanised the transfer of funds from SOCBs to SOEs by fixing the lending and deposit rates. Hence, banks were not required to compete for loans and deposit at a market-determined rate. Figure 16 portrays 3-bank and 5-bank asset concentration ratios along with the Lerner index to illustrate the competitive scenario of banking sector in China. Despite all these reforms over the years, the concentration of big three and big five banks increased substantially from 30% and 45% respectively in 2000 to 75%, and 85% in 2003, and remained almost the same until 2013. Subsequently, the concentration of these banks decreased. In 2017, the share of top three and top five banks accounted for 37% and 52%, respectively. Lerner's index, which indicates the monopoly power of banks, shows no apparent change over the years. Although regulatory restrictions from Chinese banking system abolished to a great extent, structural reforms by diminishing monopoly power of banks are required for the future to increase efficiency and innovation in the banking system.

Obviously, competition is a means by which efficiency of firms can be nurtured. However, it depends on how well bank can manage assets and labilities professionally and keep their operating costs low. It seems Chinese banks have been successful so far in managing their cost and income. For instance, the cost to income ratio of Chinese banks decreased from 71% in 1999 to 32.2% in 2017, which is substantially lower than those of Japan (69%) and the United States (57%).

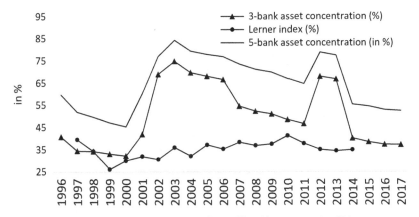

Figure 16 Market concentration of banking sector in China
Source: *Constructed based on IMF data*

We further check the relation between market concentration and stability. Figure 17 documents the relation between big 3-bank asset concentration and stability, measured by Z-score, of Chinese banks for the period 1997–2017. Higher concentration means lower competition and vice versa. The figure projects a negative association between bank's concentration and Z-score. It means that as the concentration increases (competition decreases), banks' Z-score decreases, which means that competition enhances stability of Chinese banks. They do so by squeezing operating costs as shown earlier. This finding has a significant implication for Chinese banks as some commercial banks in China enjoy natural monopoly. The government must break this monopoly and enhance competition for the greater interest of the banking sector's stability. How to enhance competition without compromising bank's resilience would be a great challenge for policymakers in China.

In 2020, Chinese government scrapped all regulatory restrictions from foreigners owning financial institutions in China. This means that banks in China are likely to face augmented competition in the future. Granted, Chinese banks can compete with foreign banks in terms of size, as they have already turned gigantic, but Chinese banks are not equally equipped with technology and skills required to compete with their foreign counterparts that have long experience of analysing and managing borrowers' credit risk. Even if local banks are comparatively in a superior position in expanding loans to mainland China than their foreign counterparts because the former can count on cultural factors, the latter's can take the advantage of technological sophistication and superior skills of screening and monitoring borrowers.

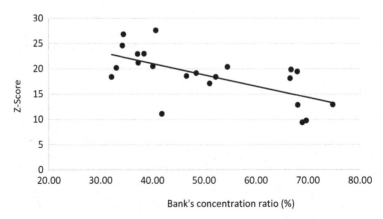

Figure 17 Market concentration vs. stability
Source: *Constructed based on IMF data*

At the same time, the presence of foreign banks will bring qualitative changes in the management of banks. For instance, accounting practices of firms need to be upgraded commensurably with foreign banks so that Chinese banks can utilize the advantage offered by a transparent and objective accounting system. The auditing practice in China is barely comparable with the Western firms because of short institutional history of audit profession in China. The Chinese Institute of Certified Public Accountants (CICPA) was established in 1988, but this professional body was remodelled to its current shape in 1995. The members of this institute increased quickly to 250,000. However, a comparatively short history of CICPA demands more time to prepare skilled CPAs required by Chinese booming enterprises including banks. Hence, Chinese banks need additional investment for developing skills and knowledge of human resources through training and development. Only then they can expect to successfully compete with foreign financial institutions.

5.4 Internationalization and the Effect of Fintech

Economic and financial reforms in China were followed by a change in the ownership structure of banks. Although the government still retains the controlling share of large banks, private shareholders have been increasing gradually. Likewise, the share of SOCBs was taken over by small commercial banks which are mostly privately owned (Figure 13). For instance, the share of JSCBs and city commercial banks in the lending market increased to 17.8% and 10.03%, respectively, in 2013 (Tan, 2020). Likewise, the share of SOCBs declined from 88% in 2007 to 55% in 2016 (Matthews and Zhiguo, 2020). This has an important repercussion on the risk and profitability of Chinese banks. In the past, government did not expect SOCBs to be highly profitable; rather, the resources were channelled to the economy through the banking system to achieve a broader goal – employment and social stability. Recent change in the ownership pattern means that banks should focus on pleasing their shareholders by chasing long-term objective – increasing firm value.

Commercial banks' attempt to look for a sustainable profit depends greatly on few interactive factors. First, banks can focus on a strategy that helps them penetrate international financial markets. Compared to other countries with similar level of financial development, Chinese banks' penetration of international market is miniscule. Stent (2017) analyses IMF data and shows that overseas loans as a percentage of total loans increased marginally from 6.15% in 2009 to 9.2% in 2013. However, if loans disbursed in Hong Kong, Macao, and Taiwan are not considered international loans, the amount of Chinese banks' overseas assets declines to half of the current level (Stent, 2017).

Moreover, technologies have revolutionized financial service industry, particularly during the COVID-19 pandemic. Considering the current disruptive nature of technology, national borders may deem to be irrelevant for financial service providers. This may cast an opportunity as well as a challenge for banks. The opportunity for banks relies on the possibility to tap technology-enabled (fintech) national and international financial markets which are growing tremendously. According to Forbes data, global digital banking amounted to US$7.7 billion in 2019 (157% growth compared to 2018), Insurtech totalled US$6.8 billion in 2019 compared to 4.4 billion in 2018, and digital payment rose to US$15.1 billion in 2019 from 12.6 billion in 2018. North American countries, especially the United States, dominate the fintech market globally, followed by Europe, the Middle East, and Pacific countries.

Among the Asia-Pacific countries, China has turned itself into a fintech hub. As per the data from Statista, the fintech industry in China grew from RMB30.78 billion in January 2014 to RMB491.59 billion in December 2019, monthly growth of 4.2% on average. Ant Financial – the world's largest fintech firm that owns Alipay – and Tencent are making enormous inroads in the financial service market in China, holding more than two-thirds of Chinese fintech market. Figure 18 exhibits the peer to peer (P2P) lending share by the type of institutions. Private enterprises are leading the P2P lending market in China. However, venture capital is emerging as a leading P2P lending institution. Innovative skills and experience in dealing with new customers provide venture capitalist with the advantage in the technology-enabled financial markets. Banks lag other competitors, no wonder because banks lend mostly depositors' money, and they must take utmost care to protect these funds. Since P2P lending market is shrouded by uncertainty and risk, Chinese banks shy away from undertaking risks involved with P2P lending.

It is too early to judge what awaits the future of fintech, but fintech has some promising features to offer. Technology-enabled firms would be able to provide more efficient banking services at a much lower cost. Philippon (2015) shows that the average cost per unit of financial intermediation in the United States remained around 2% for the last 130 years even though the use of information technology increased manifold during this time. Fintech thus, promises to break this tradition by reducing the cost of financial services and improving customers' welfare. Unlike a typical commercial bank, technology-enabled financial firms, though remain outside the purview of the formal regulation, do not shoulder the burden of additional expenses including the regulatory compliance costs, branch set-up costs, and other overhead costs. At the same time, processing of transactions using information and communication technology is faster and less complex. Hence, fintech offers customers

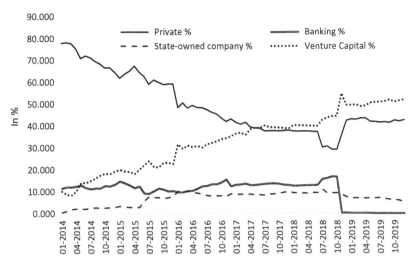

Figure 18 P2P lending market share by type of institutions
Source: *Constructed based on CEIC data*

increased value at a lower cost than the mainstream financial service providers.

Commercial banks in China must prepare themselves to face the challenge stemming from the fintech markets. They cannot simply shy away from the fintech-enabled market because fintech-enabled firms would take the advantage of low cost and simplicity in transaction processing time to attract customers and investors towards them. Such a tendency would shrink the mainstream financial markets all over the world in the future. If banks aim to compete successfully, they must invest substantially in building fintech architecture, which will create upward pressure on bank's cost. According to China's Fintech Industry Report, 2019, various financial institutions invested an estimated amount of RMB230 billion in 2018, of which about 30% were invested in big data, artificial intelligence, and cloud computing. Moreover, commercial banks must reduce their service cost while upending the quality of services. Matching these attributes for Chinese commercial banks, which were under the protective regime for a long time, would be a daunting task.

5.5 Corporate Governance Reform

One of the poorly reformed areas in Chinese financial system is corporate governance of banks. The conventional agency theory which underlies the very rationale for corporate governance of firms does not typically apply to banks in China. The principal or owners of state-owned Chinese banks, as per the laws of the land, are the people of the country. The agents are the managers like any other enterprises in the world. Hence, the principal–agent relation in the context of Chinese banks indicates the relation between people in general and bank managers. However, the state is entrusted by the citizen to carry out the role of principal on their behalf. This applies to SOCBs and JSCBs to a large extent. On the other hand, local government replaces the state as principal for city banks and RCCs. The augmented scale of principals such as state, city, and local governments is labelled as 'enhanced shareholder primacy theory' (Zou, 2019).

A typical corporate governance structure in China can be characterized by a hybrid system that combines the primacy of shareholders as well stakeholders. As mentioned before, Chinese banks are not free to function and govern themselves without the influence of the government. The foremost goal of Chinese leaders was not to ensure a better governance, but rather, to utilize the financial system to achieve greater objectives – economic development and financial stability. The governance of SOCBs was tightly knit with the smooth functioning of SOEs. Hence, governance mechanism in the early phase of economic reform was designed to serve the interest of various stakeholders including employees and the people at large. This system of corporate governance embodies the concept of stakeholder's model. Recently, Chinese banks have listed them in national and international exchanges and issued shares to public. Therefore, banks can no longer ignore the rights of dispersed shareholders and must appreciate shareholders' value. Hence, the governance of Chinese banks can be explained by a hybrid model.

Until recently, governance of banks couldn't be separated from the management because banks were instructed to concentrate on achieving objectives set by the state – accelerating economic development through financing strategic sectors identified by the state. Since the demarcation of the objectives of state and banks was blurred, it was difficult to ascertain if corporate governance in Chinese banks functioned properly. For instance, a large pile up of NPLs was an indication that corporate governance was functionally inactive. However, if banks lend to SOEs – where SOCBs' loans and NPLs are mostly concentrated – under the direction of the state, it cannot be concluded that there is an agency problem. In fact, bank's objective collided with that of the state.

Managers of banks may have achieved what the state directed them, but not always to the same degree as the state wanted. Managers have enormous discretion to shirk or seek managerial perks at the expense of the state. Nolan and Yang (2017: 5) summarize the features of corporate governance on SOCBs, ' ... plagued by not only insider control, soft budget constraints, inadequate safeguards for minority shareholders, but also political interference, lack of transparency, accountability dilution and human capital loss'. They allude to a lack of effective corporate control that can prevent cadre-manager from malpractices. This suggests that the governance mechanism in the early stage of reform focussed merely on mitigating manager's shirking behaviour by providing incentive measures.

These practices have changed to some extent over the years, slowly though. China introduced a dual board system – a board of directors and a supervisory board. The supervisory board usually enjoys less scope and power than the board of directors. Also, the supervisory board has an overlapping duty with other committees formed under the board of directors such as audit committee and risk management committee. Although a board is composed of independent, executives, and non-executive members in China, in fact, non-executive and independent members are selected mostly from the high-ranking government officials and members of the Chinese Communist Party (Luo, 2016). Moreover, the background of independent and non-executive members also does not commensurate with required business acumen and calibre. A report by Deloitte (2019) presents the board scenario of big six Chinese banks in 2017. The report shows that about 39% of the eighty-nine directors of big six banks had worked for government for a considerable amount of time. The report further shows that only 44% of the directors possessed managerial or operational experience. It is thus, questionable if independent directors can perform the duty as a whistle-blower or function as a true watchdog. The prompt answer is no because of other critical reason, the party management.

In 2004, a shareholding reform paved the way for emergence of a modern corporate governance system in Chinese banks. However, it was advised that banks, mostly SOCBs, must include 'Party Building Work' into their articles of association. By 2017, most commercial banks, especially the big banks, have complied with this instruction. This provision means that there will be a representation of party in the governance of banks. The basic idea behind introducing party committee is to meet the demand of the ruling party to control large commercial banks and play the leading role in governing banks (Deloitte, 2019). In this sense, the party committee stands above the management and the board of directors as far as making and executing corporation decisions. Deloitte further shows that 41.6% of the board members were non-executive directors and appointed by the Central Huijin Investment Co., Ltd (state-owned investment company holding majority shares of the big four banks) to represent the equity stake. These directors work full time in the banks which leaves very little room for independent directors to work for the better interest of the minority shareholders. Such a unique corporate governance model may have worked effectively in China so far. However, the country has reached a higher stage of economic development. The traditional way of governing firms may reveal its loopholes in the new normal. Unless these issues are addressed firmly and immediately, Chinese commercial banks would find it difficult to contribute successfully to the growth in the new normal.

5.6 Summary

In light of the Japanese experience, this section has attempted to identify critical determinants that may emerge as defining issues. Whether China is likely to follow Japan's fate depends greatly on how successfully China can resolve these issues without much delay. These determinants are not mutually exclusive but rather interactive. For instance, financial inclusion is essential to maintain a stable growth. Failure of mainstream financial institutions to include rural and financially stranded population leads to the rise of a 'shadow banking' or private lending market where channelling of funds takes place beyond the formal banking/financial system. Shadow banking institutions in China comprise moneylenders, trust companies, microfinance institutes, and so on. They receive deposits mostly from those small and unbanked depositors who seek quick return. Likewise, they provide loans to customers at a non-official lending rate which is higher than the formal market rate. Yao and Hu (2016) argue that some informal financial service providers work like 'Ponzi scheme' because they exploit marginal customers and hide borrowers' credit risk.

Private lending market, which amounts to about 5 trillion Yuan at present, is not only costly for borrowers but also risky and unstable. Currently borrowers of private lending market number about 80 million, most of which are SMEs. If China wants to continue the pace of stable growth in the new normal, these SMEs cannot be left out of the growth caravan. This calls for identifying the reasons as to why firms resort to private lending markets. The reasons may include systemic hindrances such as administrative complexities, higher cost of bank loans due to inefficiency and large pile up of NPLs, lending preference to region, groups, gender, firms size, and so on. Resolving such issues would be the key to chart a future reform of Chinese banking system.

Second, China has removed all formal restrictions that prohibit foreign owners from fully owning financial firms in mainland China. This implies that domestic banks are likely to face competition from foreign peers in the future. Third, technologically enabled firms are gradually making an inroad in the financial markets, which would narrow the scope of traditional lending and borrowing markets for banks. This may force banks to venture into new areas of lending and borrowing. Fourth, large three banks still hold about one-third of the total banking system's assets in China. Natural monopoly may function as a hindrance to efficiency and innovation. This suggests that further reform is essential on structural aspects, especially ownership transformation, enhancing competition, and fostering innovation. Moreover, banking sector's loan portfolio is concentrated on non-productive sectors including construction and real estate. It is believed that the real-estate sector has already reached peak in China. Hence, the elasticity of this sector to economic development has already been exhausted.

These forces are likely to change banks' risk appetite in the future. So, banks in the new normal will face dynamic and extended challenges in terms of risk management. Addressing these issues in a strategic manner would help China avoid Japan's fate.

6 Conclusion

Recent slowdown of Chinese economy after registering double-digit growth for almost three decades has raised a lot of speculations among academia and policymakers across the globe. One such speculation is whether China is destined to follow Japan's fate. Such a suspicious sketch of Chinese economic future is not completely baseless in a sense. For instance, China witnessed two external events of financial turmoil in the past. The first was the Asian financial crisis of 1996–97. The crisis crippled the financial and economic backbone of Asian emerging tigers including South Korea, Singapore, Taiwan, and Hong Kong, while other three economies – Malaysia, Indonesia, and Thailand – were practically devastated. The second wave – the GFC of 2007–09 – was much larger in scale and impact. It was initially escalated by the US subprime mortgage crisis and wreaked havoc on economies worldwide, particularly in advanced economies such as the United States, the United Kingdom, Germany, and Japan. None of these episodes affected China to a significant extent.

However, since 2012, when the world economy was relatively stable and recovering from the GFC, the GDP growth rate of China has been falling owing mainly to some internal factors. This has raised a question as to whether China has already reached maturity of productivity and growth and is on course to Japan's track. The current research has attempted to answer this question by shedding an analytical light on the banking sector of the country. Banking sector is believed to serve as a barometer to understand the future economic trajectory because a growing economy requires enormous support from the banking sector, especially in bank-based economies, to meet the nascent financing needs of corporations. On the contrary, major financial and economic crises precede a credit bubble. Hence, banking sectors cast an important insight into an economy.

To achieve the above-stated objective, the research explains major causes of Japan's banking crisis, describes banking sector reforms China has implemented so far and outlines issues that China needs to carefully address in the future. In what follows, we summarize the major findings of this research.

The guided capitalism of Japan was characterized by a strong regulation in the financial system. Although such a policy helped accelerate economic growth by facilitating easy finance for growing manufacturing sectors, Japan delayed much needed economic and financial liberalization. One of the effective tools of the government control over the financial regime was the foreign-exchange market. Keeping the value of JPY depreciated Japan provided a comparative advantage to local exporters in the international market. However, in the face of strong pressure from the United States, Japan was forced to appreciate the value of JPY after the Plaza accord in 1985. Such an appreciation proved augur ill for local exporters. To soften the pressure, Japanese government increased money supply by adopting quantitative easing policy which was not essential at all. Rather, corporations needed new ideas and innovation required to compete with international competitors. Japan's regulated economy failed to promote such techniques and ideas and suffered as a result.

Second, the main bank model of screening and monitoring, which was effective during the catching up period of Japan, became incompatible with the frontier economy. The traditional growth drivers, manufacturing enterprises, were cash-rich owing mainly to lucrative profits they enjoyed in the last two decades. Hence, they did not require external finance as much as they used to seek from banks earlier. Moreover, cheaper alternatives to bank finance were open to creditworthy borrowers. Hence, banks loosened their grips on corporation for effective monitoring. This circumstance further forced financial institutions to explore new avenues for lending. SMEs and real-estate sectors were potential but risky. Banks embarked on them. Some of these SMEs couldn't cope with the evolving uncertainty at the frontier stage and eventually failed. Banks suffered from huge NPLs once the real estate and capital markets bubble burst.

Third, the regulatory authority not only delayed the fixing of mounting NPL problems of banks but also did not show sincere willingness to resolve them. The traditional 'convoy system', which underlies the idea that all banks should progress together, resulted in deep moral hazard problems among bank managers. However, the intensity of these problems remained low during the rapid and moderate growth periods to the extent that economic growth offset the adverse effect of moral hazard without any trouble. However, once the growth slowed down, the crack appeared seriously. Regulatory authorities initially thought to manage them without letting banks fail, but such a policy was untenable due to unprecedented level of NPLs. Lack of moral and financial support forced government to allow some financial institutions to go bankrupt.

November 1997 was fateful because many highly acclaimed financial institutions were bankrupted, followed by the venerated LTCB in the following year. China obviously wants to avoid committing the same mistakes as those of Japan. Consequently, it has implemented various reforms. The following is the summary of major reforms of banks in China.

First, the 1978-reform changed Chinese banking system tremendously. The traditional mono-banking system was abandoned by introducing four new banks separating their specialized activities. Corporations, in the post-reform era, frequently resorted to commercial banks to meet their funding necessities. Alternative financing sources such as bond and stock markets were absent. The success of the reform relied on collecting deposits from households, endowed with primitive accumulation. Funds were then transferred to SOEs. Like Japan, lending and deposit rates were tightly regulated. Success of banks relied more on meeting the credit target assigned by the central government to strategic sectors than merely earning profit. SOEs were aware about the government's soft budget constraint which resulted in moral hazard. Banks couldn't recover loans disbursed to SOEs. This resulted in the pile up of NPLs in the entire banking system.

Second, Chinese government wanted to bring efficiency by enhancing competition in the banking system. This led to the launching of BOCOM which was later transformed into JSCBs. These banks were meant to cater to the needs of the regional business entities. Government found it ideal to allow more financial institutions for the interest of credit expansion. Consequently, non-bank financial institutions including securities companies, trust and investment funds, and leasing and insurance companies were allowed to operate. Notably, the introduction of rural and urban credit cooperatives was one step forward in expanding financial services to rural unbanked population.

Third, the introduction of the Commercial Bank Law of China was a landmark achievement. This law officially mandated the PBOC as the central banks of the country. The law further introduced various measures aimed at financial deepening with efficiency. Commercial banking activities were separated from investment banking activities. To ensure better governance, banks were required to introduce committee system so that lending decisions are made based on the borrower's creditworthiness. The law further recommended to classify loans as per the international loan-classification standards.

Fourth and most important reform of banking system of China was the offloading of mounting NPLs of SOCBs. In so doing, the government first introduced three policy banks to absorb the policy lending of commercial banks. Later, the government launched four AMCs where commercial banks transferred their NPLs. The Central Huijin, affiliated with MOF, managed the transfer by injecting funds into those AMCs. Commercial banks got rid of trouble loans concentrated mostly on SOEs. This was one of the strategies that paved the way for listing to exchanges and offloading shares of Chinese banks. In so doing, Chinese banks have been able to attract investment which eventually facilitates the diversification of bank ownership. In line with these reforms, China now allows fully foreign-owned financial institutions in mainland China.

These reforms are the products of several laudable endeavours from the Chinese policymakers because the country's banking system was under repression for a substantial period following the reform in 1978. We now look Chinese reform achievement through the lens of Japanese experience of banking crisis.

Like Japan, China did not resolve NPLs problem appropriately. The government just transferred NPLs from one entity (banks) to another (AMCs). The big four banks in China are state-owned. It is rational for those banks to conjecture that government would rescue them during the time of financial distress. History suggests that capital was injected time and again to replenish state-owned banks' depleted capital base. Moreover, four SOCBs are now among the top five banks in the world. These four banks share majority of the banking sector assets in China. Thus, too-big-to-fail hypothesis may worsen managerial moral hazard and influence lending decision. It is urgent for Chinese policymakers to find suitable solutions to restrict forming moral hazards in the banking system for ensuring greater stability. Restructuring banks' ownership and administrative reforms are some feasible policy options. During the catching up of Chinese economy, size may have achieved a scale effect. However, as the economy moves forward, size simply doesn't mean a lot if efficiency is compromised. This suggests that Chinese policymakers should carefully monitor the competition and efficiency nexus of banks.

Second, banks in Japan failed to cope with the fundamental uncertainty embedded with the SMEs once the manufacturing sector was financially self-reliant or found cheaper alternatives to bank finance. China is also going to face somewhat similar problem in the future. A reform in 2020 allowed foreign owners to fully own financial institutions in mainland China. On the other hand, fintech firms tend to take market share of banks away. Domestic banks can expect intense competition from foreign financial institutions to capture creditworthy borrowers. On the other hand, Chinese manufacturing sectors are gradually moving towards the frontier phase and will be cash rich soon. Maturity of this sector implies that commercial banks must make effort to find new lending opportunities. In addition, Chinese policymakers emphasize on financial inclusion for maintaining the current level of GDP growth rate. On the other hand, recent failure of many RCCs has created a financing gap for rural borrowers. It is highly likely that commercial banks in China may be strategic-ally forced to extend loans to those sectors. It is thus essential to hone screening and monitoring capabilities of mainstream banks.

Third, corporate governance remains one of the critical future reform areas for China. Japan failed to transform its old corporate governance model which was ineffective to direct firms adopting cutting-edge technology and curb moral hazard problems. Corporate governance among banks in China is not strong enough to accomplish a task that Japan failed to tackle. Independent directors are not independent in true sense as most of them are directly linked to govern-ment through various connections. Corporate takeover market, which is an important corporate governance mechanism, is practically absent. In addition, the committee system which can effectively install internal control system is rudimentary. These issues need to be addressed without further delay if China wants to avoid Japan's fate.

Finally, Chinese traditional export market, especially low-end consumer products, already reached maturity. If the country wants to avoid further decline in GDP growth, it must focus on competing internationally in the durable consumer markets. This requires a culture of creativity and innovation and ample supply of funds for innovative projects. Only an efficient financial system can help achieve this objective. If China wants to avoid Japan's path, these reforms are essential. China must decide which roads it likes to embark on.

References

Akerlof, G. A. (1970). Quality uncertainty and the market mechanism. *Quarterly Journal of Economics*, 84(3), 488–500.

Aoki, M. (1988). *Information, Incentives and Bargaining in the Japanese Economy: A Microtheory of the Japanese Economy*, Cambridge: Cambridge University Press.

Aoki, M., Patrick, H. & Sheard, P. (1994). The Japanese main bank system: An introductory overview, in M. Aoki, & H. Patrick, eds, *The Japanese Main Bank System and Its Relevance for Developing Market and Transforming Socialist Economies*, Oxford: Oxford University Press, pp. 1–50.

Baglole, J. (2004). Chinese credit ratings: a huge leap of faith. *Far Eastern Economic Review*, 8: 9–42.

Barro, R. J. (2016). Economic growth and convergence, applied to China. *China & World Economy*, 24(5): 5–19.

Beck, T., Demirgüç-Kunt, A. & Levine, R. (2001). Legal theories of financial development. *Oxford Review of Economic Policy*, 17(4): 483–501.

Berger, A. N., Hasan, I. & Zhou, M. (2009). Bank ownership and efficiency in China: What will happen in the world's largest nation? *Journal of Banking & Finance*, 33(1): 113–130.

Bloch, H. & Tang, S. H. (2003). The role of financial development in economic growth. *Progress in Development Studies*, 3(3): 243–251.

Botrić, V. & Slijepčević, S. (2008). Economic growth in South-eastern Europe: the role of the banking sector. *Post-Communist Economies*, 20(2): 253–262.

Cargill, T. F. (2000). What caused Japan's banking crisis? in T. Hoshi, & H. Patrick, *Crisis and Change in the Japanese Financial System*, Boston, MA: Springer, pp. 37–58.

Cheng, L. (2003). *Banking in Modern China: Entrepreneurs, Professional Managers, and the Development of Chinese Banks, 1897–1937*, Cambridge: Cambridge University Press.

China Statistical Yearbook. (1997). *National Bureau of Statistics China, http://www.stats.gov.cn/english/*

Claessens, S. & Laeven, L. (2005). Financial dependence, banking sector competition, and economic growth. *Journal of the European Economic Association*, 3(1): 179–207.

Coase, R. & Wang, N. (2016). *How China became capitalist*, Springer: Basingstoke.

Deloitte. (2019). *Research Report on the Corporate Governance Practices of China's Big Six Commercial Banks*, China: International Finance Corporation, Deloitte, retrieved from file:///Users/azwad/Downloads/lu-2019-corporate-governance-practices-china-big-six-commercial-banks.pdf on October 12, 2021

Diamond, D. W. & Dybvig, P. H. (1983). Bank runs, deposit insurance, and liquidity. *Journal of Political Economy*, 91(3): 401–419.

Dore, R. (2000). *Stock Market Capitalism: Welfare Capitalism: Japan and Germany Versus the Anglo-Saxons*, Oxford: Oxford University Press.

Dorn, J. (2006). Ending financial repression in China. *Global Economic Review*, 35(2): 231–238.

Feyzioglu, M. Porter, M. & Takáts, E. (2009). *Interest rate liberalization in China*. Working Paper, International Monetary Fund, https://doi.org/10.5089/9781451873184.001

Franks, J., Mayer, C. & Miyajima, H. (2014). The ownership of Japanese corporations in the 20th century. *The Review of Financial Studies*, 27(9): 2580–2625.

Fukao, K. & Yuan, T. (2018). The People's Republic of China's slowdown: Lessons from Japan's experience and the expected impact on Japan's economy, in J. Lin, P. Morgan, & G. Wan, eds, *Slowdown in the People's Republic of China: Structural Factors and the Implications for Asia*, Tokyo: Asian Development Bank Institute, pp. 61–95.

Gerlach, M. L. (1992). The Japanese corporate network: A blockmodel analysis. *Administrative Science Quarterly*, 37(1): 105–139.

Goldsmith, R. W. (1985). *Comparative National Balance Sheets: A Study of Twenty Countries, 1688–1979*, Chicago: University of Chicago Press.

Green, F. & Stern, N. (2015). China's 'new normal': Structural change, better growth, and peak emissions. *Policy Brief, London: Centre for Climate Change Economics and Policy and Grantham Research Institute on Climate Change and the Environment* retrieved from https://www.lse.ac.uk/GranthamInstitute/wp-content/uploads/2015/05/Green-and-Stern-policy-paper-March-2015a.pdf on December 12, 2021

Greenwood, J. & Jovanovic, B. (1990). Financial development, growth, and the distribution of income. *Journal of political Economy*, 98(5): 1076–1107.

Guo, Y. (2002). *Banking Reforms and Monetary Policy in the People's Republic of China: Is the Chinese Central Banking System Ready for Joining the WTO?* Basingstoke, Hampshire: Palgrave, Basingstoke.

Hellmann, T., Murdock, K. & Stiglitz, J. (1997). Financial restraint: toward a new paradigm, in M. Aoki, M., H. Kim, & M. Okuno-Fujiwara, eds, *The*

Role of Government in East Asian Economic Development: Comparative Institutional Analysis, Oxford: Oxford University Press, pp. 163–207.

Hiwatari, N. (2000). The reorganization of Japan's financial bureaucracy: The politics of bureaucratic structure and blame avoidance, in T. Hoshi & H. Patrick, eds, *Crisis and Change in the Japanese Financial System*, Boston, MA: Springer, pp. 109–136.

Ho, S. & Marois, T. (2019). China's asset management companies as state spatial–temporal strategy. *The China Quarterly*, 239: 728–751.

Hoshi, T. (2001). What happened to Japanese banks. *Monetary and Economic Studies*, 19(1): 1–29.

Hoshi, T. & Kashyap, A. (2001). *Corporate Financing and Governance in Japan: The Road to the Future*, Cambridge, MA: The MIT press.

Huang, Y. & Ge, T. (2019). Assessing China's financial reform: Changing roles of the repressive financial policies. *Cato Journal*, 39(1): 65–85.

Hutchison, M., Ito, T. & Westermann, F. (2006). The great Japanese stagnation: lessons for industrial countries, in M. Hutchison, T. Ito, & F. Westermann, eds, *Japan's Great Stagnation Financial and Monetary Policy Lessons for Advanced Economies*, Cambridge, MA: MIT Press, pp. 1–32.

Ikeda, S. (2002). *The Trifurcating Miracle: Corporations, Workers, Bureaucrats, and the Erosion of Japan's National Economy*, New York: Routledge.

Ito, T. (2000). The stagnant Japanese economy in the 1990s: The need for financial supervision to restore sustained growth, in T. Hoshi & H. Patrick, eds, *Crisis and Change in the Japanese Financial System*, Boston, MA: Springer, pp. 85–107.

Jappelli, T. & Pagano, M. (1994). Saving, growth, and liquidity constraints. *Quarterly Journal of Economics*, 109(1): 83–109.

Jensen, M. & Meckling, W. (1976). Theory of the firm: Managerial behavior, agency costs and ownership structure. *Journal of Financial Economics*, 3(4): 305–360.

Jiang, C. & Yao, S. (2017). *Chinese Banking Reform: From the Pre-WTO Period to the Financial Crisis and Beyond*, Switzerland: Springer.

Johnson, C. (1982). *MITI and the Japanese Miracle: The Growth of Industrial Policy, 1925–1975*, Stanford: Stanford University Press.

Johnson, C. (1995). *Japan, Who Governs?: The Rise of the Developmental State*, London: WW Norton.

King, R. G. & Levine, R. (1993). Finance and growth: Schumpeter might be right. *Quarterly Journal of Economics*, 108(3): 717–737.

Kornai, J., Maskin, E. & Roland, G. (2003). Understanding the soft budget constraint. *Journal of Economic Literature*, 41(4): 1095–1136.

Krugman, P. (2013). Hitting China's Wall. The New York Times, 18 July, Retrieved on 27 September 2021, from www.nytimes.com/2013/07/19/opin ion/krugman-hitting-chinas-wall.html?_r=0.

Lardy, N. R. (1998). *China's Unfinished Economic Revolution*, Washington, DC: Brookings Institution Press.

Laurenceson, J. & Chai, J. (2003). *Financial Reform and Economic Development in China*, Cheltenham: Edward Elgar.

Leland, H. E. & Pyle, D. H. (1977). Informational asymmetries, financial structure, and financial intermediation. *Journal of Finance*, 32(2): 371–387.

Levine, R. (2003). More on finance and growth: More finance, more growth? *Federal Reserve Bank of Saint Louis*, 85(4): 31–46.

Li, L., Willett, T. D. & Zhang, N. (2012). The effects of the global financial crisis on China's financial market and macroeconomy. *Economics Research International*, http://doi.org/10.1155/2012/961694, retrieved from https:// downloads.hindawi.com/archive/2012/961694.pdf on November 25, 2022

Li, W. & Yang, D. (2005). The great leap forward: Anatomy of a central planning disaster. *Journal of Political Economy*, 113(4): 840–877.

Livingston, M., Poon, W. P. & Zhou, L. (2018). Are Chinese credit ratings relevant? A study of the Chinese bond market and credit rating industry. *Journal of Banking & Finance*, 87: 216–232.

Luo, D. (2016). *The Development of the Chinese Financial System and Reform of Chinese Commercial Banks*, Basingstoke: Palgrave Macmillan.

Lou, J. (2000). China's bank non-performing loan problem: Seriousness and causes. *The International Lawyer*, 34: 1147–1992.

Mabuchi, M. (1995). Financing Japanese industry: The interplay between the financial and industrial bureaucracies, in H. K., Kim et al., eds., *The Japanese Civil Service and Economic Development: Catalysts of Change*, Oxford: Clarendon Press, pp. 288–310.

Matthews, K. & Zhiguo, X. (2020). Rational cost inefficiency and convergence in Chinese banks. *Economic Modelling*, 91: 696–704.

McKinnon, R. I. (1973). *Money and Capital in Economic Development*, Washington, DC: Brookings Institute.

Miah, M. D. & Uddin, H. (2017). Hostile takeover in Japan: Institutional constraints and change. *International Journal of Business and Globalisation*, 19(1): 6–26.

Morck, R. K. & Nakamura, M. (2005). A frog in a well knows nothing of the ocean: A history of corporate ownership in Japan, in R. Morck, ed, *A History of Corporate Governance Around the World: Family Business Groups to Professional Managers*, Chicago: University of Chicago Press, pp. 367–466.

Murach, M. & Wagner, H. (2017). How severe will the growth slowdown in China caused by the structural change be? An evaluation based on experiences from Japan and South Korea. *Journal of Chinese Economic and Business Studies*, 15(3): 269–287.

Murphy, R. T. (1989). Power without purpose: the crisis of Japan's global financial dominance. *Harvard Business Review*, 67(2): 71–83.

Nakano, M. (2016). *Financial Crisis and Bank Management in Japan (1997 to 2016)*, London: Palgrave Macmillan.

Noguchi, Y. (1995). The role of the fiscal investment and loan program in postwar Japanese economic growth, in Hyung-Ki, Kim et al., eds, *The Japanese Civil Service and Economic Development: Catalysts of Change*, Oxford: Clarendon Press, pp. 261–287.

Nolan, P. & Yang, X. (2017). *The Political Economy of Banking Governance in China*, London: Routledge.

Ogura, S. (2002). *Banking, the State and Industrial Promotion in Developing Japan, 1900–1973*, Basingstoke: Palgrave.

Okazaki, K. (2007). *Banking system reform in China: The challenges of moving toward a market-oriented economy*. Rand National Security Research Division, retrieved on 3 September 2021, from www.rand.org/pubs/occasio nal_papers/OP194/

Okimoto, D. (1989). *Between MITI and the Market: Japanese Industrial Policy for High Technology*, Stanford: Stanford University Press.

Patrick, H. (1966). Financial development and economic growth in underdeveloped countries. *Economic Development and Cultural Change*, 14(2): 174–189.

Pempel, T. (1998). *Regime Shift: Comparative Dynamics of the Japanese Political Economy*, Ithaca, London: Cornell University Press.

Perkins, D. (1994). Completing China's move to the market. *Journal of Economic Perspectives*, 8(2): 23–46.

Philippon, T. (2015). Has the US finance industry become less efficient? On the theory and measurement of financial intermediation. *American Economic Review*, 105(4): 1408–1438.

Prowse, S. (1992). The structure of corporate ownership in Japan. *Journal of Finance*, 47(3): 1121–1140.

Roach, S. (2016). Is China the Next Japan, *Project Syndicate*, 27 June 2016. Retrieved from https://www.project-syndicate.org/commentary/no-lost-decades-for-china-by-stephen-s--roach-2016-06 on November 20, 2021

Rumbaugh, T. & Blancher, N. (2004). China: International trade and WTO accession. *IMF Working Papers*, 036, https://doi.org/10.5089/9781451845 488.001

Schmidt, D. (2009). The financial crisis and its impact on China. *China Analysis Research Group on the Political Economy of China*, 67, 1–4

Shang, M. (2000). *Fifty Years of Monetary Finance in New China*, Beijing: China Finance & Economics Publishing House.

Shaw, E. S. (1973). *Financial Deepening in Economic Development*, New York: Oxford University Press.

Smith, R. C. (2016). Is China the next Japan? *The Independent Review*, 21(2): 275–298.

Song, L. (2018). State-owned enterprise reform in China: Past, present and prospects. In R. Garnaut, L. Song, & C. Fang, eds, *China's 40 Years of Reform and Development: 1978–2018*. Canberra: ANU Press, pp. 345–376.

Stent, J. (2017). *China's Banking Transformation: The Untold Story*, Oxford: Oxford University Press.

Stiglitz, J. E. (1994). *Whither Socialism?* Cambridge, MA: MIT Press.

Stiglitz, J. & Weiss, A. (1981). Credit rationing in markets with imperfect information. *American Economic Review*, 71(3): 393–410.

Suzuki, Y. (2011). *Japan's Financial Slump: Collapse of the Monitoring System under Institutional and Transition Failures*, Basingstoke: Palgrave MacMillan.

Suzuki, Y. & Miah, M. (2017). China's 'New Normal': An interpretation from institutional and Marxian views. *Journal of Comparative Asian Development*, 16(1): 21–46.

Suzuki, Y., Miah, M. & Yuan, J. (2008). China's non-performing bank loan crisis: The role of economic rents. *Asian-Pacific Economic Literature*, 22(1): 57–70.

Tan, Y. (2020). Competition and profitability in the Chinese banking industry: New evidence from different ownership types. *Journal of Industry, Competition and Trade*, 20(3): 503–526.

Ueda, K. (2000). Causes of Japan's banking problems in the 1990s, in T. Hoshi & H. Patrick, eds, *Crisis and change in the Japanese Financial System*, Boston, MA: Springer, pp. 59–81.

Vogel, E. (1979). *Japan as Number One: Lessons for America*, Cambridge: Harvard University Press.

Vogel, S. (2006). *Japan Remodeled: How Government and Industry are Reforming Japanese Capitalism*, Ithaca and London: Cornell University Press.

Wang, H. (1999). The Asian financial crisis and financial reforms in China. *The Pacific Review*, 12(4): 537–556.

Wang, Q., Stephen, Z. & Ernest H. (2010). Chinese economy through 2020: It's not whether but how growth will decelerate, *Morgan Stanley China Economy*, Morgan Stanley Research Asia/Pacific, 20 September.

Yafeh, Y. (2000). Corporate governance in Japan: Past performance and future prospects. *Oxford Review of Economic Policy*, 16(2): 74–84.

Yamamura, K. (1995). The role of government in Japan's 'catch up' industrialization: A neoinstitutionalist perspective, in H. K., Kim, et al., eds, *The Japanese Civil Service and Economic Development: Catalysts of Change*, Oxford: Clarendon Press, pp. 102–134.

Yamamura, K. (2018). *Too Much Stuff: Capitalism in Crisis*, Bristol: Policy Press.

Yamori, N. & Sun, J. (2019). How did the introduction of deposit insurance affect Chinese banks? An investigation of its wealth effects. *Emerging Markets Finance and Trade*, 55(9): 2022–2038.

Yang, D. (1996). *Calamity and Reform in China: State, Rural Society, and Institutional Change since the Great Leap Famine*, Stanford: Stanford University Press.

Yao, W. & Hu, J. (2016). Inherent risks in Chinese shadow banking, in A. Sheng, & N. Soon, eds, *Shadow Banking in China: An Opportunity for Financial Reform*, West Sussex: John Wiley and Sons, pp. 133–170.

Yao, Y. (2014). A New Normal, but with robust growth: China's growth prospects in the next 10 years, *THINK TANK 20: Growth, Convergence and Income Distribution: The Road from the Brisbane G-20 Summit*, The Brookings Institute, 77–82, Retrieved from https://www.relooney.com /NS4053/TT20%20Nov%207%20FINAL%20Web%20v2.pdf#page=5

Yao, Y. (2018). Will the People's Republic of China be able to avoid the Japan syndrome? in J. Lin, P. Morgan & G. Wan, eds, *Slowdown in the Peoples' Republic of China: Structural Factors and the Implications for Asia*, Tokyo: Asian Development Bank Institute, pp. 30–60.

Yeung, G. (2009). How banks in China make lending decisions. *Journal of Contemporary China*, 18(59): 285–302.

Yusuf, S. (1994). China's macroeconomic performance and management during transition. *Journal of Economic Perspectives*, 8(2): 71–92.

Zou, W. (2019). *Corporate Governance in the Banking Sector in China*, Singapore: Springer.

Cambridge Elements ☰

Economics of Emerging Markets

Bruno S. Sergi
Harvard University

Editor Bruno S. Sergi is an Instructor at Harvard University, an Associate of the Harvard University Davis Center for Russian and Eurasian Studies and Harvard Ukrainian Research Institute. He is the Academic Series Editor of the Cambridge *Elements in the Economics of Emerging Markets* (Cambridge University Press), a co-editor of the *Lab for Entrepreneurship and Development* book series, and associate editor of *The American Economist*. Concurrently, he teaches International Economics at the University of Messina, Scientific Director of the Lab for Entrepreneurship and Development (LEAD), and a co-founder and Scientific Director of the International Center for Emerging Markets Research at RUDN University in Moscow. He has published over 150 articles in professional journals and twenty-one books as author, co-author, editor, and co-editor.

About the Series

The aim of this Elements series is to deliver state-of-the-art, comprehensive coverage of the knowledge developed to date, including the dynamics and prospects of these economies, focusing on emerging markets' economics, finance, banking, technology advances, trade, demographic challenges, and their economic relations with the rest of the world, as well as the causal factors and limits of economic policy in these markets.

Cambridge Elements ≡

Economics of Emerging Markets

Elements in the Series

Printed in the United States
by Baker & Taylor Publisher Services